THE EXPECTANT FAMILY

From Pregnancy through Childbirth

By Fairview Health Services
Affiliated with the University of Minnesota

Fairview Press
Minneapolis

Published by Fairview Press, 2450 Riverside Avenue, Minneapolis, Minnesota 55454. Fairview Press is a division of Fairview Health Services, a community-focused health system affiliated with the University of Minnesota and providing a complete range of services, from the prevention of illness and injury to care for the most complex medical conditions. For a free current catalog of Fairview Press titles, please call toll-free 1-800-544-8207, or visit www.fairviewpress.org.

Library of Congress Cataloging-in-Publication Data
The expectant family : from pregnancy through childbirth / by Fairview Health Services.
   p. cm.
This volume was first published as part of Caring for you and your baby:
from pregnancy through the first year of life, 1997.
Includes index.
   ISBN 1-57749-145-9 (trade paperback : alk. paper)
1. Pregnancy. 2. Childbirth. I. Fairview Health Services.
RG525.E985 2004
618.2'4--dc22   2003016046

First printing: January 2004
Printed in the United States of America
08 07 06 05 04   6 5 4 3 2 1

Writer: Linda Picone
General editor: Lora Harding-Dundek
Book designer: Jane Dahms Nicolo
Illustrator: Barbara Beshoar

Acknowledgments
Many individuals from Fairview Health Services contributed to this project. They include Dalia Abrams, BSc, MA, CCE; Jody Arman-Jones, BsEd, CCE; Nancy Barkley, RN; Judy Cannon, RNC, MS; Deb Cathcart, RN, MS; Linda DiBartolo, RNC; Kathy Eide, RN, NP; Mary Ess, RN, IBCLC; Donna J. Florence, MS, RN, ACCE, CNS; Patricia Fontaine, MD; Laurie Frattallone, BA; Becky Gams, RNC; Kay Gray, BA, BS; Judy Grumm, RN; Margaret Harder, CCRN, BSN, MA; Lora Harding-Dundek, BA, MPH, ICCE; Jeanne Hartwig, LPN; Debra Heaver, RN; Jane Helgesen, RN, IBCLC; Debra Johnson, RN; Kathryn Kerber, RN, MS, CNS; Evelyn Lindholm, RN, IBCLC; Kathleen Maloney, RN; Rachel McCann, RN; Laurie McNamara, RN; Bonnie Miller, RN; Patti Mortland, RN, CNNP; Kim Mullon, RN; Sue Nesheim, RN; Denise Palmer, RN, MS; Lorina Patterson, parent advisor; Vicki Pieper, RN, IBCLC; Jeri Price, BA, CCE; Wendy Raisir, parent advisor; Jane Rauenhorst, MALP; Marie Root, RN, IBCLE; Ann Shelp, BSN, ICCE; Anthony Shibley, MD; Arlyce Shook, RNC; Noreen Siebenaler, RN, MSN, IBCLC; Patti Sollinger, MSN, CPNP; Sheryl Lynds Stowman, MDiv, ACPE Supervisor; and Aner Vladaver, MD. We thank our patients and their families and the many other people who helped move this book from conception to reality.

Contents

Introduction

This book—together with its companion volume, *The New Family: Your Child's First Year*—is designed to provide the basic information you need to make the best decisions possible about pregnancy, labor, birth, and parenting. For additional information, you will find recommended resources listed at the end of most chapters.

You may, at times, feel overwhelmed with all the information and resources available to help you prepare for and parent your baby. You may wonder, "What is it that I need to know?"

To answer this general question, try to imagine yourself in specific situations:

- Do you picture yourself continuing to work and exercise during your pregnancy? If so, what information do you need in order for this to happen?

- Where do you picture yourself during labor? Are you in bed or walking? In your own clothes or a hospital gown? Who is with you? What information do you need to make these images clearer?

- Once your baby is born, do you imagine yourself and your baby together throughout your hospital stay, or is the baby in the nursery? How do you picture yourself feeding your baby?

Thinking about specific situations such as these will lead you to ask the questions that you really need answered. Together, both *The Expectant Family* and *The New Family* will bring clarity to your thoughts and help you find the answers to your questions.

In addition to the advice offered in these books, you will also receive information and guidance from health care providers. Health care providers may include physicians, certified nurse-midwives, nurses, or nurse practitioners. You may also spend time with a childbirth educator or doula. The relationships you form with the people providing direct care to you and your baby are very important. Together, these health care providers will give you the resources you need to have a healthy pregnancy and a healthy baby.

You're Pregnant

Throughout your pregnancy you will need to pay special attention to your health, for both your sake and your baby's sake. Exercise, diet, and other habits are important to how you feel during the pregnancy and for giving your baby the best start in life.

This book will take you through your entire pregnancy and the birth of your baby. The chapters are ordered in the way your pregnancy will proceed, so you can turn to each chapter to read about how your body is changing, how your baby is developing, and what you may be feeling.

SOME OF THE QUESTIONS ANSWERED IN THIS CHAPTER INCLUDE:

- What can I expect from my health care provider?
- How can I get the most from clinic visits?
- Can I drink alcohol while I'm pregnant?
- What should I eat?
- How much weight should I gain?
- Can I exercise?
- Why am I so moody?
- What if I feel overwhelmed?
- Is sex safe during pregnancy?

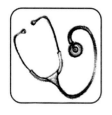

YOU AND YOUR HEALTH CARE PROVIDER

THE HEALTH CARE PROVIDERS at your clinic can help you have a better pregnancy and a healthier baby—if you start seeing them as soon as you think you are pregnant. It is important to follow their recommendations as the months go by.

You may choose a doctor, a nurse practitioner, or a nurse-midwife as your primary care provider during your pregnancy.

- Your **doctor** may be an **obstetrician**, who specializes in caring for women through pregnancy and birth, or a **family practice physician**, who can provide most health care for all members of a family.

- **Certified nurse-midwives** are registered nurses with training in pregnancy and childbirth. They provide complete prenatal care, deliver babies, and perform well-woman visits, including Pap smears and family planning. Certified nurse-midwives work closely with obstetricians and will work with you as a partner in your care.

- **Nurse practitioners** are registered nurses who have had special training in women's health. They often work with doctors during a pregnancy, and you may see a nurse practitioner frequently during your clinic visits. They do not deliver babies, but they are responsible for routine care before and after birth.

- **Physician's Assistants (PAs)** have special medical training to help doctors provide care in many different areas, including pregnancy and childbirth.

At first, you probably will visit the clinic once a month or so. Later in your pregnancy, you will be asked to come in more often, since things may change very quickly at that point. Your blood pressure, urine, and weight will be checked each time you come to the clinic. As the baby develops, its growth, heart rate, and position in your body also will be checked.

The visits to the clinic will help most women feel comfortable with their health and their baby's health. But if there are any complications, these regular visits will let your health care

What can I expect from my health care provider?

provider find them early, which is always important in preventing and treating problems.

Your health care providers are the experts when it comes to pregnancies, but you are the expert when it comes to *you*. Don't be afraid to tell them what you're thinking or feeling or worrying about. They need to know. Think of yourself and your health care providers as a team, working together toward a successful pregnancy and a healthy baby.

To make sure your visits to the clinic are most helpful, you should:

- **Write down any questions you have before your visit.** Keep a notebook or a writing pad handy. When you think of a question, write it down. Then, when you visit the clinic, you won't forget it.

- **Ask again if you don't understand an answer.** Medical words and phrases can sound odd or even frightening to patients. Repeat any question, or parts of it, if you don't understand the answer. Your health care providers want to make sure you get the information you need.

- **Be honest.** It's very, very important that you level with your health care providers about your activities—including the ones that may embarrass you. If you smoke or use drugs or alcohol, be honest. Your health care providers will help with education and referrals.

- **Describe how you're feeling as clearly as you can.** Don't just say "it hurts"; say *where*, and *how much*, and *how often*, and *when*. Sometimes it's not easy to describe, but try to be specific.

- **Keep track of what you learn during office visits.** Take notes during your office visits. It's easy to forget what you've just heard, or to get confused when you get a lot of information at once. Write it down. Keep a chart of your weight, blood pressure, and other tests (see the Keeping Track section, pages 53 to 58, for a place to do this).

How can I get the most from clinic visits?

- **Get more information.** Bookstores and libraries contain many excellent books on having a baby. At the end of each chapter in this book, you'll find a list of books, videos, and other resources you might find helpful.

WHAT YOU HAVE A RIGHT TO EXPECT

Your health care providers should give you good medical services in a respectful manner. This includes:

- **Prompt service.** You can expect to spend some time in the waiting room, but let the staff know—calmly—if you feel that you've been sitting too long. Also, expect your health care provider to return telephone calls in a reasonable time.
- **Commitment.** You should be able to receive care even when your nurse-midwife or doctor is out of town. Ask your clinic for details.
- **Respectful treatment.** You and your health care providers should have an open, honest, friendly, and respectful relationship. If you feel that you are not being treated respectfully, talk about it with your health care provider.
- **Strict regard for confidentiality.** Your visits to the health care provider and your discussions with him or her are private. Your health care provider should not talk about you with any other patients.
- **Sensitivity to cultural differences.** We're not all alike in our beliefs and habits, and your health care providers should understand and respect your cultural and ethnic background. If there are misunderstandings, it may be simply that your health care provider is not familiar with your culture. You can help educate him or her.

HEALTH INSURANCE

You are responsible for knowing how much medical coverage your insurance company will provide. It is best to call your insurance company early in your pregnancy to find out when your prenatal benefits begin, which services are covered, which health care providers you may see, and so forth. See page 31 for a list of questions to ask your insurance company.

NUTRITION AND HEALTH

YOUR BABY deserves a healthy start. Eating right, staying away from harmful substances, and exercising regularly during your pregnancy are good for your baby—and for you.

SMOKING

Is it okay to smoke while I'm pregnant?

Even if you know someone who smoked through her pregnancy and who has a healthy baby, the evidence is clear: Smoking is bad for babies. If you smoke, being pregnant is the best reason in the world to stop. Women who smoke during their pregnancy are more likely to have babies that are premature, weigh less than 5 1/2 pounds, or are stillborn or die as infants. These are frightening facts. Why take a chance with your baby? Your health care provider can help you with a program to quit smoking.

ALCOHOL

Can I drink alcohol while I'm pregnant?

"But my mother drank while she was pregnant with me and I turned out fine," you may say. It's hard to believe that something that is so much a part of our lives—a beer at a ball game, a glass of wine with dinner, champagne to celebrate a special occasion—can be dangerous to your unborn baby.

Drinking during pregnancy can cause **Fetal Alcohol Syndrome (FAS)**, a combination of birth defects that includes mental retardation. Fetal Alcohol Syndrome is the leading cause of retardation in the United States.

No one knows exactly how much alcohol during pregnancy is too much. Some studies have shown that even a small amount on a regular basis can affect the growth of a baby. Why take chances? The Surgeon General has recommended that pregnant women not drink *any* alcohol.

If you have had an occasional drink—maybe before you knew you were pregnant—you probably don't need to worry. However, you should talk to your health care provider, just to make sure.

ENVIRONMENTAL HAZARDS

Some environmental chemicals—including chemicals in the home or workplace, as well as mercury and PCBs in fish—may present a risk to your baby. Consult your care provider about potential environmental hazards. Furthermore, if you have a cat, ask someone else to change its litter box. Cat feces can be infected with **toxoplasmosis,** a parasite very harmful to your baby.

DRUGS

Any drugs, whether illegal substances like marijuana, prescription drugs, or even over-the-counter medications as ordinary as aspirin, can have an effect on your baby. You need to talk honestly with your health care provider about what kinds of medications or drugs you take.

Most illegal drugs, including cocaine, heroin, speed, ecstasy, downers, LSD, and PCP, can seriously harm your baby during pregnancy. They may cause long-term effects, including mental, physical, and emotional problems for the new baby.

Over-the-counter medications and prescription drugs may be safe, but you need to ask your health care provider about them to be sure. Some things that are usually just fine, such as aspirin, can be dangerous when you're pregnant. Make a list of everything you take, from vitamins to prescribed antibiotics to pain relievers, and share it with your health care provider.

Herbal remedies may also have an effect on your body or your baby. If you use herbs as medicine or frequently drink herbal teas, check with your health care provider for safety recommendations.

EATING RIGHT

There will be times, during your pregnancy, when you'll feel like eating everything in sight, and other times when the thought of food will make your stomach lurch. Whether you're eating a lot or a little, you should eat the right foods. Pregnancy is a good time to develop healthy eating habits, for yourself and for your family.

The Food Pyramid shown here gives the essentials of a healthy diet. A pregnant or nursing mother needs plenty of calcium, and should have at least 3 to 4 servings of dairy products each day. If you don't like milk, try yogurt or cottage cheese.

In addition to calcium, pregnant women need folic acid, which has been shown to reduce the occurrence of some birth defects. Folic acid, a compound in the vitamin B family, can be found in leafy green vegetables, fresh fruits, liver, food yeasts, cereals, breads, and peanuts, or it can be taken as a supplement.

The Food Pyramid

The pyramid is a guide for what to eat each day. Try to eat more of the foods in the bottom three parts of the pyramid. You need food from every group each day to have a well-balanced diet.

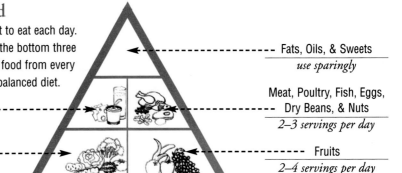

Fats, Oils, & Sweets
use sparingly

Milk, Yogurt, & Cheese
3–4 servings per day

Meat, Poultry, Fish, Eggs, Dry Beans, & Nuts
2–3 servings per day

Vegetables
3–6 servings per day

Fruits
2–4 servings per day

Grains, Cereals, Rice, & Pasta
6–11 servings per day

U.S. Department of Agriculture. U.S. Department of Health and Human Services.

Here's what different kinds of food do for you and your baby:

- **Dairy products** (milk, cheese, yogurt)—help build strong bones and teeth.
- **Protein** (meat, fish, eggs, soybeans, nuts, peanut butter)—aids brain and organ development.
- **Citrus** (oranges, grapefruit, lemon juice)—builds strong body cells and blood.
- **Leafy green vegetables** (spinach, broccoli, cabbage)—help your baby's bones, hair, and skin develop properly.
- **Other fruits and vegetables** (potatoes, carrots, apples, grapes, berries)—help prevent constipation and give you energy.
- **Bread, cereal, pasta, carbohydrates**—promote nervous system development.
- **Water and other fluids** (but not soda or coffee)—8 to 10 glasses or more each day prevent dehydration.

What should I eat?

When you're hungry, you may be tempted to reach for snacks like cookies, cake, or ice cream. Your body is telling you that it wants to eat, but it isn't telling you what to eat. You decide that, and you can make healthy decisions.

Keep healthy snacks handy. An orange can give you a sense of being full, and it's good for you and your baby. A glass of apple juice is better than a can of soda; plain crackers are better than potato chips. (Crackers, cereal, and toast often help with nausea.)

You are going to gain weight when you're pregnant, and you need to for your baby's healthy development. You may not like the way you look, especially if you've worked hard to keep a slim figure. Remember that a healthy pregnant woman looks different from a healthy *non*-pregnant woman.

If you are underweight, you will need to gain more (28 to 40 pounds) than if you are overweight (15 to 25 pounds). Average-weight women should gain 25 to 35 pounds. Eat sensibly and you should gain the amount that's right for you. An extra 300 calories a day over a healthy non-pregnant diet is just about right.

During the first three months, you may gain only a few pounds (3 to 6), most of it from the increase in your blood and fluids. During the rest of your pregnancy, you may gain as much as a pound a week as the baby grows.

A weight gain of 25 to 35 pounds during pregnancy is average. Part of this weight comes as the baby grows inside you (7 1/2 to 8 1/2 pounds) and the rest as your body changes to allow the baby to grow and as it prepares for breastfeeding the baby after birth.

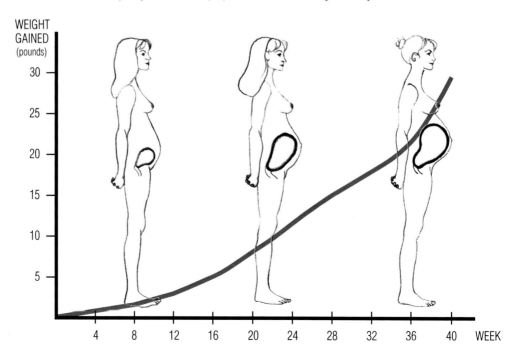

EXERCISE

REGULAR EXERCISE during pregnancy is not only good for your
baby, it will help you feel better, too. It will give you energy,
make you feel better about yourself, reduce stress—and help you
get back in shape faster after the baby is born.

Can I exercise?

If you already exercise regularly, you can probably continue
what you are doing, but at a slower pace, until your baby is
born. Check with your health care provider if your regular exercise is extremely strenuous or involves jarring movements. If
something starts to feel uncomfortable, pay attention to the signal your body is sending and substitute another kind of exercise.

If you have not been exercising regularly, start gradually and
don't suddenly try to do anything too strenuous. Walking briskly for
30 minutes or more, at least 3 times a week, is excellent exercise.

Consult with your health care provider before starting any
exercise program. Whatever exercises you do, make your movements flowing, rather than sharp or punching. Stop if you feel
pain. And always remember to drink plenty of water.

The following exercises are particularly good for pregnant
women.

Kegel

Deliberately squeeze together the muscles you use when you stop a stream of urine.
(One way to do this: Imagine that you are sitting on the toilet and the phone rings.)
Hold the squeeze for a few seconds, then release. Do this as often as possible, even
100 times a day. You can do Kegels anywhere. Doing Kegels will increase the tone
of your pelvic floor muscles, which will be especially important when your baby

puts pressure on your bladder.
It will decrease your chances
of leaking urine when you
cough or sneeze. It can
enhance lovemaking, too.
It's the most important exercise
for pregnant women.

STRONG PELVIC
FLOOR MUSCLE

WEAK PELVIC
FLOOR MUSCLE

Pelvic Rock

Get on your hands and knees. Look at your knees, pull your hips in, and arch your back like an angry cat. Hold the position for a few seconds (try counting to 5), then release. Repeat at least 10 times. This exercise helps stretch out your lower back at the end of a long day of standing.

Don't let your back arch or your tummy sag in this position.

Tailor Sit

Sit in a butterfly position with feet touching. Put your arms between your legs and drop your knees toward the floor. Count to 10, then release. Repeat at least 10 times. This exercise strengthens and stretches your inner thigh muscles.

Try not to slouch. Your lower back should remain straight.

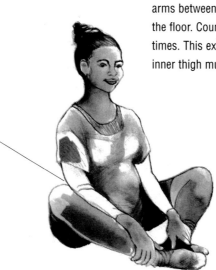

Shoulder Rotation

Put your arms straight out and make circles at your sides. Rotate 5 times in one direction, then 5 in the other direction. You can also do shoulder rotations with your hands touching your shoulders. These exercises will relieve tension in your upper back if you work at a desk or computer all day.

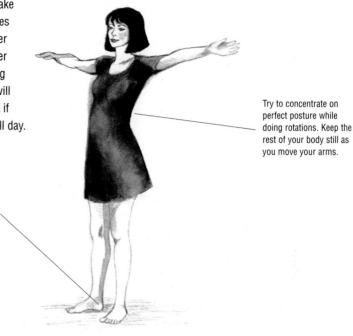

Try to concentrate on perfect posture while doing rotations. Keep the rest of your body still as you move your arms.

Feet should be about shoulder-width apart.

Back Flattening

Lie on your back with your arms at your sides. Pull your knees to your chest and cross your ankles. Press the small of your back to the floor and rotate your hips. Make circles in one direction for a few moments, then in the reverse direction. This exercise should not be done after 20 weeks of pregnancy, but in the first few months it can help relieve backaches.

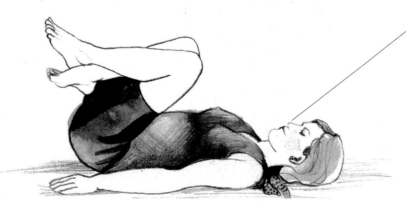

Keep breathing while doing any exercise(s). It is important for you and your baby to keep air circulating through your bodies.

YOUR EMOTIONS

BEING PREGNANT and having a baby will change your life in ways you may not be able to imagine. It's normal to have a lot of different feelings and different moods throughout your pregnancy. Sometimes you will feel happy, on top of the world. At other times you will burst into tears at the smallest thing. You may be impatient and irritable one moment, mellow and peaceful another. Sometimes you'll feel everything—happy, sad, irritable, peaceful—almost at the same time.

Why am I so moody?

Some of these mood swings are the result of hormonal changes. It helps to remember that they are normal.

Having a good sense of humor about it all will help you and those around you. Think of having this baby as an adventure, and enjoy the changes in your body and your outlook on life.

Physical changes can affect your mood. If you're feeling nauseous and tired during the first months of your pregnancy, for example, it's likely that you're going to be a bit touchy, too. When your body is bigger and you have a hard time getting out of a chair toward the end of your pregnancy, you may feel impatient, as if the baby will never be born.

If this is your first baby, you may be unsure of just what having a baby will mean to you. Some questions you may wonder about include: Is my home big enough? Will I need to give up my job? Can I take care of a baby by myself? What will labor and delivery be like? Do I have enough money? How will my relationship with my partner change? Will I love my baby enough? Will my baby love me? Talking about these issues will help relieve anxiety and let you laugh at the silly questions while finding answers to the serious questions.

If you've had children already, you may be more confident about some things—you know how to change a diaper and feed a baby, for example—but there will be other concerns. Do I have enough energy for another child? How is my partner going to react? Will my other children resent this baby? Do I have enough love to go around?

During the first three months of your pregnancy, you're likely to look inward, to feel protective of the baby inside you and to think about what he or she is going to mean to your life. The second three months are often a period of looking outward. Your pregnancy shows, you feel good physically, and you're likely to be excited about it all. Then the last three months are another period of looking inward. The weight of your baby may be slowing you down a bit, and you know that it's only a short time until you will have a child to care for.

For some women, it helps to write fears and happy thoughts in a journal during their pregnancy. Some find that just talking to other mothers relieves much of their anxiety. Some read everything they can about having a baby because being well-informed makes them feel more confident.

If this pregnancy was unplanned, if you don't have a caring partner or a support system, or if you are planning to place your baby for adoption, you will need extra emotional support. Talk to your health care provider, who can direct you to agencies and groups that will help.

STRESS

You can cope better with the stress in your life—including the stress of being pregnant—if you:

- **Eat a healthy, well-balanced diet.**
- **Get enough sleep.** Listen to what your body tells you; take a nap when you need to.
- **Get regular exercise and fresh air.**
- **Pace yourself.** Take time to relax. Don't try to do everything.
- **Enjoy yourself.** Do at least one thing every day that makes you feel good.
- **Let others help you.** Your partner or others may offer to take care of the things you normally do. Let them.
- **If you are having trouble handling the stress in your life, talk to your health care provider, who can help you find support in the clinic, hospital, or community.**

What if I feel overwhelmed?

Many pregnant women see themselves as a miracle in progress. Consider the miracle of two people uniting to form one being, cells being called together from secret places and being organized in unique and wonderful ways. You may wonder about the miraculous power that directs these amazing changes, and feel humbled in the face of such power. You may wonder why you were chosen to love and nurture this little one. All this may well lead you to believe that you are taking a spiritual journey.

Whenever you have the opportunity, you may wish to find quiet moments to relax and reflect on the profound implications of this miracle. Many expectant parents find that prayer or meditation, journaling or quiet introspection are helpful on their journey. This is a time when many people spend time thinking about God, or whomever they name as their Higher Power. Acknowledge your emotions as you journey. There may be excitement, confusion, or fear. You may feel profound awe at the mystery of creation and the Creator. You may feel anxiety and fear, question whether you are prepared for this new life, and desire to search for meaning and purpose in your own life. And you may recall those women who have gone before you on this journey—your mother, grandmothers, aunts, and others with whom you feel connected.

Your partner's life is changing, too. Preparing for this baby together can be a wonderful experience, but it can also mean a time of working through issues that you may not have discussed before. You have a right to expect support and some special attention during your pregnancy, but remember that your partner has emotional needs, too. Often partners don't feel the reality of the pregnancy as quickly as the woman whose body is changing.

Communication is essential. Talk about what you are feeling and listen to your partner's feelings. Set aside time for the two of you during the pregnancy so that you can share your excitement and your fears in an unstressed, unrushed way.

SEXUALITY

For most pregnancies, it's safe to have sex, even up through the last few weeks before the baby is born. But you, or your partner, may find your interest in sex changing during the pregnancy.

You may not be very interested in sex during the first three months of your pregnancy simply because your breasts are sore or you're tired or nauseated. During the second three months, you are likely to have more energy and you may feel very sexy with your enlarged breasts and more sensitive genital area. In the last three months of pregnancy, the size of the baby may make sexual intercourse seem awkward.

Your partner's interest in sex may mirror your own; when you feel positive and interested, your partner is likely to feel the same. Some partners find a pregnant woman to be lovely and sensuous in her growing body. But sometimes your partner may have other fears or concerns. Will sex hurt the baby? Are you now a mother and not a lover?

What matters is how you feel and how your partner feels. Now is an important time for you to be gentle and considerate with each other. If one of you is interested in sex and the other is not, you can explore other ways of being intimate, from massage or cuddling to touching until you have an orgasm.

In some situations, your health care provider may advise you not to have intercourse, or to restrict the kind of sex you have. These situations include:

- **A history of miscarriage.**
- **Vaginal infection.**
- **Vaginal or abdominal pain.**
- **Vaginal bleeding.**
- **A possibility of preterm labor.**
- **Membranes that have ruptured or are leaking.**

DOMESTIC ABUSE

PREGNANCY SOMETIMES INCREASES the abuse by a partner. It is reported that 25 to 40 percent of all abused women are abused during pregnancy.

Is sex safe during pregnancy ?

It can be hard to leave a relationship, even if you are being emotionally or physically abused, especially if you are pregnant. You may worry about whether you can support yourself on your own or you may wonder if you could raise a child without a partner.

There is no excuse for abusing a woman and her unborn baby. If you are in a relationship that is abusive, even if your partner only loses control "once in a while," you need to think about your baby as well as yourself now. Abused pregnant women are more likely to have complications during their pregnancies, including miscarriage, babies with low birth weight, hemorrhaging, early labor, and the unborn baby's death.

No one deserves to be abused. Not you or your baby. (Or your partner: occasionally, women abuse their partners.)

There are many agencies and services to help you—and your partner—avoid abuse and create a safe environment for your baby. Talk to your health care provider for a referral.

Warning Signs

When you're pregnant, some of the changes in your body can feel strange. Most of the time these changes are a normal part of pregnancy, even if they're different than anything you've felt before. But sometimes they can be signs of problems. Tell your health care provider if at any time during your pregnancy you see or feel:

- **A change in your vaginal discharge.** This means *any* bleeding from the vagina, or an increase in vaginal discharge before the 36th week (or about a month before your baby is due).
- **A sudden decrease in the baby's movement.** Your clinic may teach you how to count your baby's movements. You'll find a place to keep track of your baby's kicking and other movements on pages 53 through 58.
- **Sharp abdominal pain, or pain that doesn't seem to go away.**
- **Unusual health problems.** These can include:
    Severe nausea, vomiting, or headache.
    Swelling of hands or face, or very noticeable swelling of feet or ankles.
    Blurred vision, seeing spots in front of your eyes.
    Pain or a burning feeling when you urinate.

A decrease in the amount of urine you pass.

Chills or fever.

- **A feeling that something isn't quite right.** Even if you can't figure out exactly what it is, trust your body and your instincts.

GENETIC COUNSELING AND TESTING

GENETIC COUNSELING and testing helps families know more about whether they are likely to have a child with birth defects. They also can help find a pattern of genetic disorders in your family, if there is one. Genetic counseling and testing is not routine, but your health care provider may feel that it's recommended, especially if:

- **You are 35 or older.**
- **You have had a child with a birth defect.**
- **Your family has a medical history of genetic disorders.**

Usually, genetic testing is recommended *before* you decide to have a baby if there is a concern that you or the baby's father may carry a particular genetic condition, or if there is any family history of genetic disorders.

After you become pregnant, genetic counseling and testing may be suggested as you make decisions about the pregnancy and care of your baby after he or she is born.

An increased risk for having a baby with certain birth defects, such as Down syndrome or spina bifida, can be shown by testing a sample of the pregnant woman's blood. If the blood sample indicates an increased risk, the health care provider may recommend an **ultrasound exam** for a more definite result. For further testing, your health care provider may suggest an amniocentesis. An **amniocentesis** is the withdrawal of a small amount of the amniotic fluid that surrounds your baby. This fluid can be tested in a laboratory to give more accurate information about your baby and any genetic health risks.

If genetic tests are recommended, your health care provider will tell you how they will be done and if there are risks to your baby so you can make an informed decision. Keep in mind that most babies are born with no serious birth defects. Even when a risk of a birth defect is found, a normal pregnancy is still most likely.

FOR PARTNERS

YOU MAY BE as excited and happy as your pregnant partner. Maybe you're even *more* excited and happy. You and your partner are entering a new stage of your relationship. It means a chance to make the relationship even stronger.

You might also feel a little overwhelmed. You are expected to be supportive of your partner, but you may have your own doubts and fears to contend with.

Try to remember the good feelings you have. Preparing for a baby can be a way to grow closer. Make sure you talk to your partner. Tell her about your hopes and dreams for the baby and for both of you. Then be sure to listen to what she's telling you as well. She's likely to go through many emotions throughout the pregnancy. Enjoy the good times and be patient with any blue periods.

Keep your sense of humor, but make sure you're laughing *with* your partner, not at her. She can burst into tears at the slightest comment. Don't take it personally.

Sex can be a tricky issue during pregnancy. You may be interested when she's not, or she may be interested when you're not. Be patient, and think of ways to be close if you aren't having intercourse.

Be supportive of your partner's developing healthy habits, and join her in them. Eat well with her, exercise with her, stop drinking. If you smoke, now is the time to stop. Secondhand smoke is harmful to both mother and baby. Every baby deserves to come into a healthy home.

FOR MORE INFORMATION

A Child Is Born by Lennart Nilsson.
Active Birth by Janet Balaskas.
The Birth Partner by Penny Simkin.
Essential Exercises for the Childbearing Year by Elizabeth Noble.
Pregnancy, Childbirth, and the Newborn by Penny Simkin, et al..
Pregnancy Day by Day by Sheila Kitzinger and Vicky Bailey.
While Waiting by George E. Verrilli, MD, and Anne Marie Mueser.

The First Three Months

Your body changes very quickly during the first three months (each three months is called a **trimester**) of your pregnancy as it adapts to carrying a baby. You're likely to feel many of these changes, even though they are not usually visible to others. At the same time, your baby is growing from a single cell into an embryo that is beginning to move its limbs.

SOME OF THE QUESTIONS ANSWERED IN THIS CHAPTER INCLUDE:

- How is my baby growing?
- What can I do about "morning sickness?"
- Why do I have to go to the bathroom so often?
- What should I do for headaches?
- What are the signs of miscarriage?
- What kinds of tests will I have at the clinic?

Your Baby's Development

YOUR BABY'S life starts with just one egg in your body, joined with one sperm cell from the father. Less than an hour after these two cells have merged into one, they have begun to divide and multiply. First this looks simply like a cluster of cells, nothing like a baby. As the cells continue to multiply, they start to become specific parts of the human body.

A woman may not know yet that she's pregnant during the first month, but the baby is already growing rapidly. By the end of the first month, your baby's heart begins to beat and other organs are starting to develop. The baby is about 3/16 of an inch long, and there are dark spots where the eyes will later be.

During the second month the baby's brain and spinal cord are developing. The baby's head seems big, compared to the rest of the body. By the end of this month, the baby is about an inch long and weighs less than 1/10 of an ounce. Fingers and toes are just starting to develop.

The baby's length triples during the third month, up to about 3 inches. Now the baby weighs about an ounce. Fingers and toes are developed, and fingernails and toenails are beginning to form. There are even the beginnings of what will become the baby's teeth. The sex organs are now visible.

How is my baby growing?

 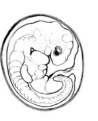 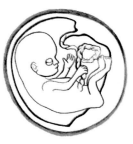 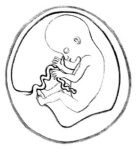

The sperm (with tail) is absorbed by the egg, or ovum, in the fallopian tube. The tail drops off, and the new combination of both the mother's and father's genetic material begins to multiply. Within a couple of hours, there are two cells. These each split and become more cells and then more. In just 5 days, there is a cluster of 90 cells.

At 4 weeks, the embryo is taking on shape, with a head and the beginning of what will be eyes.

At 8 weeks, the facial features are forming, and the baby has fingers and toes. In fact, the beginnings of all body parts and functions are now present. At 8 weeks, the embryo becomes a "fetus."

At 12 weeks, the baby's heart is complete, and the skeleton is beginning to form. The baby's proportions are close to what they will be at birth, with the head about 1/3 the size of the body.

WHAT'S HAPPENING TO YOUR BODY

YOUR BODY is changing a great deal, very quickly, during the first trimester, and it's natural for that to cause discomfort at times. Pay attention to the signals your body is sending—if you feel tired, for example, it's telling you to rest—and remember that you are likely to feel better during the second trimester.

Some of the physical changes you may experience include breast tenderness, nausea and vomiting, tiredness, faintness, frequent urination, headaches, and vaginal discharge.

BREAST TENDERNESS

For many women, sore and tender breasts are what tells them they are pregnant. Your breasts are preparing to feed a baby, so the milk glands are enlarging and the amount of fatty tissue is increasing. Your nipples may get darker and wider, and you may notice bluish veins under the skin on your breasts.

You may need to use a larger bra now, or one that is more supportive than what you've worn before. There are maternity bras, which have wide straps and backs, but any supportive bra may work for you. Cotton bras are best because they let your skin breathe.

NAUSEA AND VOMITING

If only it were just "morning" sickness! You can feel sick to your stomach anytime during the day or night, and some women say they are queasy nearly all the time during the first trimester of their pregnancy.

The good news is that this discomfort usually only occurs during the first trimester.

What can I do about "morning sickness?"

Some things that may help:
- **Keep crackers nearby and nibble a couple when you start to feel queasy, or before you get out of bed in the morning.**
- **Eat small meals several times a day so your stomach is never empty.**
- **Eat slowly.**
- **Eat a little lean meat or cheese before going to bed.**
- **Wait until after eating to drink fluids.**

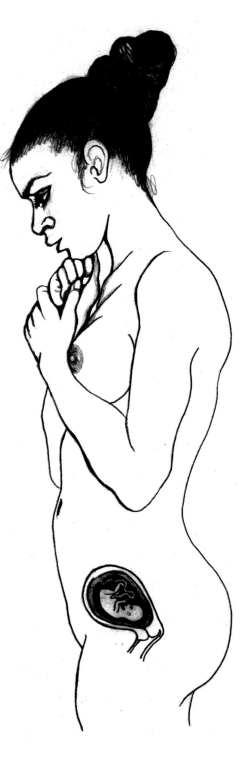

You may not "look pregnant" to others by the end of the third month, but your tummy is beginning to round as your uterus fills up more of your pelvic cavity. Your baby is about 4 inches long now.

- Avoid foods that often trigger nausea for pregnant women, such as fried foods, spicy foods, seafood, citrus juices, or drinks with caffeine like coffee, tea, and cola.
- Avoid very hot or very cold temperatures in what you drink and in your home or office.

If your nausea is severe or constant, talk to your health care provider about things that may help, including vitamin B6 or wheat germ. Very few women have nausea so severe that they need hospital care.

TIREDNESS

It's normal to feel very tired during the first few months of your pregnancy. This tiredness is caused by the dramatic changes in your hormones during this time.

It may be hard, especially if you have a job or other children, but when you feel tired, you should try to rest. Go to bed earlier than you usually do and take naps whenever you can.

Regular exercise usually does not make you more tired—just the opposite. Exercise stimulates circulation and is good for you and the baby. Walking is particularly good, and it's usually easy to fit into your routine.

During your pregnancy, you may be more likely to develop **anemia**. When you are anemic, your blood does not carry oxygen to the rest of your body the way it should. Your tiredness may be at least partly caused by anemia. Talk to your health care provider about severe tiredness.

FAINTNESS

During the first few months of your pregnancy you may suddenly feel dizzy or faint when you stand up after sitting or lying down. Or you may get faint after standing for a long time, especially in a warm room. This faintness may be caused by low blood pressure, low blood sugar, or anemia.

If you feel faint, sit and put your head down between your knees. Get up slowly, if you've been sitting or lying down. If you have to stand for a while, move around and exercise your legs.

Eating 5 or 6 small meals throughout the day can help keep up your blood sugar.

FREQUENT URINATION

As your uterus grows with the baby, it presses on your bladder and you need to go to the bathroom more often. Most women notice this most during the first few months and then again during the last few months.

You need to drink plenty of fluids—8 to 10 glasses (8 ounces per glass) or more each day—to stay healthy during your pregnancy, but you can drink most of it earlier in the day so you won't have to get up to go to the bathroom many times during the night.

Kegel exercises (see previous chapter) can strengthen your pelvic muscles to control your urine so you don't "dribble" at embarrassing moments.

Why do I have to go to the bathroom so often?

HEADACHES

When you feel a headache starting, lie down in a dark, quiet room if you can. A hot or cold compress (like a washcloth) at the back of your neck may help.

Most health care providers think that acetaminophen (Tylenol) is safe to take during pregnancy. Do not take aspirin or ibuprofen without first consulting your health care provider.

Talk with your health care provider if your headaches are longer or stronger than usual or your vision changes. This kind of headache is sometimes a sign of high blood pressure, and you and your baby may need special care.

What should I do for headaches?

VAGINAL DISCHARGE

Your vaginal discharge may change several times during your pregnancy. You may be more prone to yeast infections or other vaginal infections. Your health care provider can give you medication, which will not harm your baby, to treat these infections. Do not douche during pregnancy, and do not use any suppositories, such as yeast medication, without talking to your health care provider. You may want to avoid perfumed soap, toilet tissue, and talcum powder. Wear only cotton panties.

MISCARRIAGE

MORE THAN 20 percent of all pregnancies end in miscarriage, usually during the first trimester. Often there's no apparent reason for a miscarriage, but probably it is because your body recognizes that something is not going well with the development of the baby or the pregnancy and begins a natural process to end the pregnancy.

Even though it is natural and common, miscarriage can be a very difficult loss for a woman and her partner. You've been looking forward to this baby, you've started to dream about what it will mean to be parents, you may have told your friends and relatives . . . and now those lovely dreams are gone. You may feel guilt. Did I do something wrong? Can I get pregnant again? Will I lose another baby if I do?

Your health care provider can help give you answers to these questions that are specific to you and your pregnancy. It's very unlikely that you did anything to cause the miscarriage. Exercise, sex, strong emotions, or even a bad fall rarely cause miscarriage. Having a miscarriage, even if it's not your first, doesn't necessarily indicate anything about your ability to become pregnant again or to carry a baby to the normal end of pregnancy. However, your body may need to rest and heal before you become pregnant. Your health care provider can advise you on when it is safe to try again.

SIGNS THAT YOU MAY BE HAVING A MISCARRIAGE

If you have any of the following signs, you should call your health care provider immediately. You may be told to stay home and watch your symptoms, or you may be told to come in right away.

What are the signs of miscarriage?

- **Bleeding or spotting.** Pink or brown discharge, less than during a period. Spotting in the first months of pregnancy doesn't necessarily mean that you will have a miscarriage, but it's a symptom you should pay attention to.
- **Cramping.** Some cramping similar to what you feel during a menstrual period is normal, but cramping and bleeding together may signal a miscarriage.

- **Heavy bleeding.** Bright red blood, as heavy as a menstrual period or more.
- **Intense cramping.** You may feel continuous cramps, or very heavy ones that come and go. This is much more painful than the cramps you may have had with your period.
- **Passing of large clots.** A white or gray clot along with larger blood clots may mean you already have had a miscarriage. You should save the pregnancy tissue and show it to your health care provider.

CLINIC VISITS

YOUR FIRST VISIT will be longer and more involved, and you may want to have your partner with you so both of you can ask questions.

Your height, weight, and blood pressure will be taken. (Your weight and blood pressure will be taken on every visit to the clinic during your pregnancy.) Your health care providers will take a health history and ask you questions about diet, habits, and family medical history.

The health care provider will examine your ears, eyes, nose, throat, heart, lungs, breasts, abdomen, and lymph nodes. You will have a pelvic exam to check your vagina, cervix, uterus, fallopian tubes, and ovaries. The size of your uterus will be measured to help determine just how many weeks pregnant you are. If you are far enough along, your health care provider will listen for your baby's heartbeat. A Pap test will be done to screen for abnormalities or signs of cervical cancer.

You will be asked for samples of blood and urine so that laboratory tests can be done. Your blood type, Rh factor, and iron count will be checked. Your blood will be tested for certain sexually-transmitted diseases that can affect your baby, and for whether you have had German measles or have been exposed to hepatitis. You will also be offered an HIV test. Your urine will be checked for the levels of sugar and protein, and for any infection.

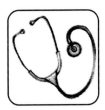

What kinds of tests will I have at the clinic?

Ultrasound

An ultrasound may be given during your first or second trimester. It is not a routine test and will be done only if your health care provider feels it is medically necessary. The ultrasound uses high frequency sound waves to produce a picture of your baby.

The procedure is simple: You lie down and your abdomen is covered with a gel. Then the health care provider passes a transducer, or special microphone, over your abdomen. Usually you and the health care provider can watch the image on a screen as the transducer is moved. You may be given a "picture" of your baby to take with you.

Your health care provider may use the ultrasound to check:

- **The number of babies.**
- **The location of the placenta.**
- **The estimated due date.**
- **The baby's weight.**
- **The baby's growth and development.**

QUESTIONS TO ASK YOUR INSURANCE COMPANY

WHEN YOU call your insurance company, explain that you want to verify your obstetric or maternity benefits, and that you need the following information.

Date/Time of call _____ Insurance company _____

Person you spoke to _____ Policy number _____

1. On what date do my prenatal benefits begin? _____

2. Does my policy cover education for birth, breastfeeding, and parenting? _____

3. Am I assigned to a specific primary care clinic? _____

4. Are there any copayments? Is there a deductible or out-of-pocket maximum? Does the out-of-pocket maximum include the deductible? _____ _____

5. If my baby is the grandchild of the policy holder, is the baby eligible for insurance coverage? ___ yes   ___ no

6. Does my hospital stay need to be pre-approved? ___ yes   ___ no
   If yes, what do I need to do to receive pre-approval? _____

7. If I have an uncomplicated vaginal birth, how long can I remain in the hospital before I need a doctor's authorization to stay longer? _____

8. If I have an uncomplicated cesarean birth, how long can I remain in the hospital before I need a doctor's authorization to stay longer? _____

9. Does authorized hospitalization begin with admission or time of delivery?
   ___ admission   ___ time of delivery

10. Is additional hospitalization time authorized if there are complications?
    ___ yes   ___ no

11. If I have a son and desire circumcision, is circumcision covered? ___ yes   ___ no

12. What coverage is provided if my baby requires additional hospitalization?

    _____

13. Am I authorized to stay in the hospital as long as my baby is hospitalized?
    ___ yes   ___ no

14. Does my coverage include home visits by a registered nurse? ___ yes   ___ no

15. What is the process for adding my new baby to my insurance policy?

    _____

16. Will I be notified if my benefits change? ___ yes   ___ no

FOR PARTNERS

THIS IS a good time to learn more about pregnancy. The two of you might even read some books together, so you both understand what she is going through. There's a lot both of you may not know, especially if this is a first pregnancy.

The more you share in the pregnancy, the better she is likely to feel. Go with her to the health care provider, at least for the first visit. (If you can, go every time.) Ask your own questions.

Do more around the house. She really is tired. Her body is doing a lot of work that you can't see, and she needs plenty of rest. A little pampering goes a long way toward having a healthier pregnancy and baby.

You may feel like this newly-pregnant person is not the woman you know. She's tired much of the time, she's running to the bathroom every 15 minutes, she's throwing up, she doesn't want to be touched. . . .

The best thing you can do is be patient. Understand that this is all normal—and it doesn't last for very long.

If the pregnancy ends in a miscarriage, encourage her to talk about what it means to her—and be sure to talk about your own feelings as well. Most couples need some time to grieve this loss.

FOR MORE INFORMATION

Our Stories of Miscarriage by Rachel Faldet and Karen Fitton.
A Child Is Born by Lennart Nilsson.
Active Birth by Janet Balaskas.
The Birth Partner by Penny Simkin.
Essential Exercises for the Childbearing Year by Elizabeth Noble.
Pregnancy, Childbirth, and the Newborn by Penny Simkin, et al.
Pregnancy Day by Day by Sheila Kitzinger and Vicky Bailey.
While Waiting by George E. Verrilli, MD, and Anne Marie Mueser.

The Second Three Months

The fourth, fifth, and sixth months of pregnancy are often the "golden" time for many women. Any queasiness and tiredness you felt earlier are gone, you have more energy—and you're finally starting to *look* pregnant. You also begin to feel the movements of your developing baby.

SOME OF THE QUESTIONS ANSWERED IN THIS CHAPTER INCLUDE:

- How is my baby growing?
- What's happening to my body?
- Is it normal to feel blue?
- How do I prepare my other children for a new baby?
- What tests will my health care provider do?

YOUR BABY'S DEVELOPMENT

BY THE BEGINNING of the fourth month, your baby's heartbeat can be heard with a stethoscope. The brain looks like an adult's, but smaller. The baby is about 8 1/2 inches long, weighs 6 ounces, and has eyebrows and eyelashes. Many babies begin to suck their thumbs about now.

How is my baby growing?

During the fifth month, right around 20 weeks, you will begin to feel your baby's movements. This used to be called the "quickening," meaning that the baby had just come to life. Actually, your baby has been moving for quite a while but was too small for you to feel it before. Now the baby's twists and turns cause you to feel an odd, butterfly-like sensation in your abdomen. By the end of the fifth month, your baby weighs about a pound and is about 12 inches long.

A protective covering called **vernix** develops during the sixth month of pregnancy. This cream cheese-like material will stay on your baby right through birth, protecting his or her skin from drying. Your baby's skin is reddish and wrinkled now. The baby's eyes are open and sensitive to light. The ears are developed, and your baby can hear sounds. It's a good time to have conversations, even to sing, to the baby inside you.

Your baby is already an individual, with unique fingerprints and footprints, by the end of the sixth month. He or she is about 14 inches long and weighs about 2 pounds.

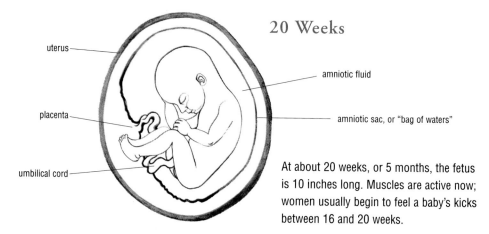

20 Weeks

uterus

amniotic fluid

placenta

amniotic sac, or "bag of waters"

umbilical cord

At about 20 weeks, or 5 months, the fetus is 10 inches long. Muscles are active now; women usually begin to feel a baby's kicks between 16 and 20 weeks.

WHAT'S HAPPENING TO YOUR BODY

FINALLY, you look pregnant. Your breasts are large (although they may not have grown any more since the first couple of months), and your belly is rounded. Most women begin wearing maternity clothing sometime during the second trimester of their pregnancy.

Whether you wear maternity clothing or not, make sure that you choose clothing that is comfortable and that doesn't bind you.

Physically, the second trimester of pregnancy often is a "golden" time. The nausea of early pregnancy usually ends before or during the fourth month and all of a sudden you are *hungry*. The fatigue caused by your hormonal adjustment is gone, and you may feel very energetic.

Keep healthy food around to satisfy your hunger—fruit and raw vegetables, not salty snacks. Eating a balanced diet may have been difficult during the first trimester, when you were often queasy. Now is a good time to make sure you're eating well.

Some physical changes you may experience during the second trimester of your pregnancy include:

HEARTBURN

As your baby grows, your stomach gets squeezed and stomach acid may back up the esophagus, causing a burning sensation in your upper abdomen. Eating frequent small meals, rather than large ones, helps. Don't lie down right after eating, and sleep with your head propped up, to keep the stomach acid from backing up. Talk to your health care provider about antacids if changes in your diet don't help.

CONSTIPATION

Hormones make your digestive system work more slowly, and constipation is a common problem during pregnancy. You can ease constipation by drinking lots of fluids, eating high fiber foods, such as bran, raisins, and raw vegetables and fruit, and getting regular daily exercise.

What's happening to
my body?

12 to 16 Weeks   16 to 20 Weeks   20 to 24 Weeks

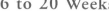
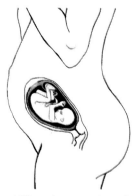

By 4 months, you probably have gained about 9 pounds. Less than 2 pounds of that is the baby, the placenta, and the amniotic fluid; the rest is accounted for by the increased blood volume and fat tissue that prepares you to nurse your baby.

Around 20 weeks, your uterus is about level with your navel, and your abdomen is swelling. If others haven't noticed you were pregnant before, they are likely to now.

The skin on your abdomen is stretching as your baby grows, and you may see red streaks, or stretch marks, on your belly. If your skin is light, these marks will fade to a silver color after your baby is born. If you have dark skin, the marks will stay dark.

SKIN CHANGES

Changing hormones may change your skin. You may develop blemishes—or any blemishes you have may clear up. Some women get a darkening of the skin on their face or abdomen. Dry, itchy skin is common. A good skin care routine will help some of these problems. Clean your skin with a mild soap (don't use deodorant soap) and warm—not hot—water. Follow with a good moisturizer. One that is unscented is less likely to cause itching. Remember that these skin problems will go away after the baby is born.

ROUND LIGAMENT PAIN

The ligaments that help support the uterus are stretching as your baby grows, which can sometimes cause a sharp pain on one or both sides of the uterus. You may feel this pain when you cough, sneeze, or make quick movements. This pain is common about the fifth month of pregnancy but can also happen later. If you feel a pain, bend toward the side that hurts or pull your knee toward your chest. A warm pack or hot water bottle may also help.

PREPARING FOR BREASTFEEDING

IF YOU THINK you would like to breastfeed your baby, you can begin preparing your breasts now to help make your early breast-feeding experiences pleasant and comfortable.

The best preparation for breastfeeding is to eat a well-balanced, healthy diet, to get enough sleep, and to learn how to relax. Your body will do the rest.

You should:

- **Keep your breasts clean, but wash only with warm water.** Your nipples have special glands that make a substance that helps keep your nipples soft and protects against infection. You don't want to wash it off with soap.
- **Support your breasts with a good bra.** If you normally are small-breasted, you may need to purchase a bra that gives you more support. This doesn't mean lots of wires or uncomfortable ribbing, but something made from natural fibers—like cotton—with wide straps.

EMOTIONS

THE SECOND TRIMESTER of pregnancy is a time when you are likely to feel focused outward. You are beginning to look rounder, so others may comment on your pregnancy, giving you advice and congratulations. You have more energy, so you are likely to be doing more than during the first trimester. It can be a very happy time.

As you start to feel your baby move, the fact that your life is going to change with this new baby becomes very real. Some days that may feel wonderful; on other days it may feel frightening. It's normal to have the blues sometimes, even when everything is going well.

It's important to talk about your concerns with others—your partner, friends, family, and health care providers. If you don't have support, your health care providers can refer you to agencies and services that may help.

Is it normal to feel blue?

SPIRITUALITY

This may be a very joyous time in your life, and you may be looking forward with great anticipation to the birth of your child. However, you may also have concerns and even experience a sense of loss from time to time. You may wonder if you will be able to cope with the stress of labor, the demands of parenting, and the changes in your relationships. Having a baby means letting go of the old to make way for the new. Letting go can bring sadness and anxiety, but also joy and freedom. Take time to reflect on these feelings. It may be helpful to consider your relationship with God, the Creator, or your Higher Power. This relationship can help you gather your strength and wisdom for the journey ahead. Many expectant parents find that their spiritual life is enriched and deepened during this time of change.

YOUR OTHER CHILDREN

YOU MAY HAVE waited to talk about the new baby coming, but now you're starting to look different and other adults are talking about the baby. It's usually a good time to share the news with your other children.

How do I prepare my other children for a new baby?

Emphasize the positive—"You're going to be a brother or sister"—rather than what they may see as an intrusion—"You're going to have a new brother or sister." Remind them, every day, that you love them by telling them, by hugging and cuddling, by giving them your attention.

The following are some ways to help your children accept the idea of a new baby:

- **Talk about the baby with them. Let them feel the baby's movements.**
- **If you're going to make major changes, like putting them in a different bedroom, don't do it right before the birth.**
- **Read books about new babies with your children.**
- **Show them pictures of themselves when they were first born, and talk about that time.**
- **Take them for tours of the birthing area, so they will know where they can visit you.**

CLINIC VISITS

YOU PROBABLY will see your health care provider about once a month during this part of your pregnancy.

Your weight, blood pressure, and urine will be sampled during each visit. The health care provider will listen to the baby's heart, measure the baby's growth, and ask about the baby's movements. Some tests may be recommended during this period, including:

TRIPLE SCREEN TEST

This blood test is done to screen for Down syndrome and for abnormalities in the spinal cord. The test can be done at any-time between 15 and 21 weeks into the pregnancy, but the best time is 16 weeks.

The triple screen is not a required test, but it is offered to everyone. It's really a combination of three tests: alpha-fetoprotein (AFP), unconjugated serum estriol, and human chorionic gonadotropin (HCG). The AFP can indicate possible spinal cord abnormalities; all three tests are needed to determine the risk for Down syndrome.

The triple screen test predicts the risk of abnormality, not whether your baby actually has an abnormality. If the risk is high, other tests will be offered to diagnose any problem.

ULTRASOUND

An **ultrasound** may be given during your first or second trimester. It is not a routine test and will be done only if your health care provider feels it is medically necessary. The ultrasound uses high frequency sound waves to produce a picture of your baby. (See page 30 for more discussion of an ultrasound test.)

AMNIOCENTESIS

This test is used to diagnose certain genetic disorders or, later in pregnancy, to check on other aspects of the baby's health.

A local anesthetic is used to numb the skin on your abdomen. A thin needle is then inserted through your abdomen and a small amount of amniotic fluid is withdrawn to be tested in a lab. There is a risk to the baby with this test, so it is only done if medically necessary. Your health care provider will discuss the procedure and its risks with you, if amniocentesis is suggested.

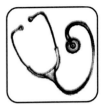

What tests will my health care provider recommend?

What is an ultrasound?

CHILDBIRTH CLASSES

IT'S TIME to look into the variety of childbirth preparation classes and to sign up. The staff at your clinic can refer you to the classes that are right for you.

FOR PARTNERS

ENJOY THIS "golden" period of the pregnancy with your partner, but remember that she still needs a little extra care. It's a good time for both of you to do some of the planning for the arrival of the new family member. You might decorate the baby's room, get some of the equipment you will need (a car seat, a crib, a stroller), and start investigating for daycare.

One of the best things you can do for your partner now is to support and encourage her in developing a healthy lifestyle. Take walks with her, plan healthy meals, go grocery shopping and help select healthy snacks rather than fatty, non-nutritive ones. It will be good for both of you.

If there are already children in the home, help reassure them that they are loved. Encourage them to talk about the baby. Listen to their fears and concerns about the baby.

Sign up for and make plans to attend childbirth classes with her. And in the meantime, attend as many clinic visits with her as you can.

FOR MORE INFORMATION

Active Birth by Janet Balaskas.
The Birth Partner by Penny Simkin.
A Child Is Born by Lennart Nilsson.
Essential Exercises for the Childbearing Year by Elizabeth Noble.
Having Twins by Elizabeth Noble.
The Multiple Pregnancy Sourcebook by Nancy Bowers.
Pregnancy, Childbirth, and the Newborn by Penny Simkin, et al.
Pregnancy Day by Day by Sheila Kitzinger and Vicky Bailey.
While Waiting by George E. Verrilli, MD, and Anne Marie Mueser.

Maternity Wise <www.maternitywise.org>.

4 *The Final Three Months*

You're getting bigger—you may think you're *huge*—and you can't wait for this baby to arrive. At the same time, you may be nervous and even a little sad about the end of this stage of your life. There are lots of things to do before the baby arrives, so this is a very busy time for you.

SOME OF THE QUESTIONS ANSWERED IN THIS CHAPTER INCLUDE:

- How is my baby growing?
- Is it normal for my feet to swell like this?
- What do I do to get ready for the baby?
- What if I'm placing my baby for adoption?
- How often will I see my health care provider?

DURING THE LAST trimester of pregnancy, your baby is growing and getting stronger. Although the baby's organs and systems are developed, they need these final weeks to mature before a healthy birth. A premature baby born at the end of the seventh month may live, but one born at the end of the eighth month is even more likely to live.

By the end of the eighth month, your baby may weigh as much as 5 pounds and be 18 inches long. At the end of the ninth month, an average full-term baby weighs about 7 1/2 pounds. Yours may be even heavier.

You may feel your baby hiccuping during the last 8 to 10 weeks of pregnancy, as well as kicking and pushing heavily against your abdomen.

During the ninth month, the baby's head drops into your pelvis as the preparation for birth begins.

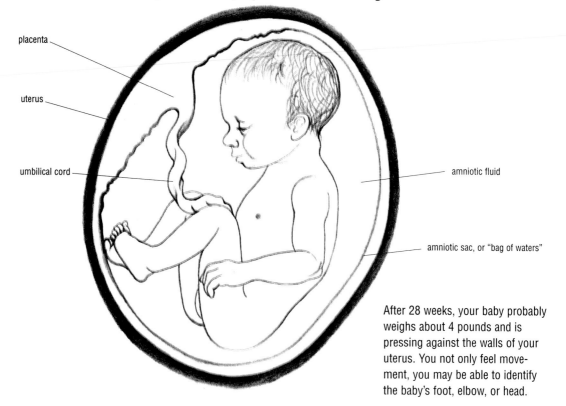

placenta

uterus

umbilical cord

amniotic fluid

amniotic sac, or "bag of waters"

After 28 weeks, your baby probably weighs about 4 pounds and is pressing against the walls of your uterus. You not only feel movement, you may be able to identify the baby's foot, elbow, or head.

What's Happening to Your Body

JUST GETTING UP out of a chair may feel like a big deal during the last month or two of your pregnancy. Your baby is getting big, and you may feel awkward. Sleeping may be harder because you can't find a comfortable position. Your feet get tired. As the baby drops into birth position, your bladder is squeezed and you have to go to the bathroom more frequently.

Most of the physical difficulties in the last trimester of pregnancy are the result of the increasing size of the baby—and you. Some things you may experience include:

Backache

You tend to walk, stand, and sit differently when you're pregnant, and this can strain the muscles in your back. Sometimes the baby's head may press against your spine, causing a lower backache. Try to keep your shoulders straight, and avoid wearing high heels.

Frequent Urination

The baby's position changes in late pregnancy and puts pressure on your bladder, so you will need to urinate more frequently. Don't hold your urine; this can cause a bladder infection. Keep drinking plenty of fluids, and try to empty your bladder fully whenever you urinate.

Contractions

The muscles of your uterus tighten and relax frequently during your pregnancy, although you usually can't feel the contractions until the fourth month or later. Sometimes referred to as **Braxton-Hicks contractions**, these irregular contractions do not get stronger and are not signs of labor. You can continue your normal activities, especially walking. (For more information on early contractions, see the section on preterm labor beginning on page 49.)

Varicose Veins

Your slower circulation and the pressure of your growing baby can cause **varicose veins**, usually later in pregnancy. Avoid standing for long periods, do not sit with your legs or ankles crossed, and try to rest a few times each day with your legs up. Your health care provider may recommend elastic stockings.

24 to 28 Weeks   28 to 32 Weeks   32 to 36 Weeks

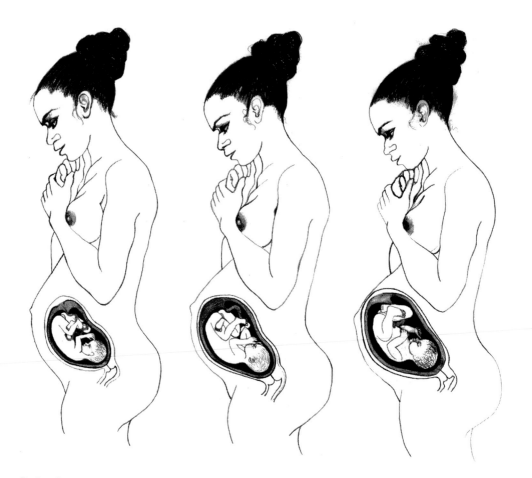

During these last months, your baby may nearly double in weight. You are heavier, not just from the baby, but from an increase in body fat and blood volume. The baby's head presses against your bladder, which causes you to go to the bathroom more often, and the baby's bottom presses against your diaphragm, making you short of breath.

HEMORRHOIDS

Your baby's growth, and the increase in your blood supply
during pregnancy, put pressure on the veins in your rectum. Many
women develop hemorrhoids. You can help avoid them by eating
foods that will keep you from getting constipated. Kegel exercises
(see page 11), which strengthen the muscles of your anus as well as
your vagina, may also help. If you do get hemorrhoids, try using
an ice pack, tub bath, or cloth soaked with cold witch hazel. Avoid
sleeping on your back, which can aggravate hemorrhoids. Ask
your health care providers about medications that might help.

LEG CRAMPS

Leg cramps usually happen while you're in bed. Your body
doesn't absorb calcium as well when you're pregnant, and this lack
of calcium can cause muscle cramps. Eating and drinking foods
with calcium—dark green leafy vegetables, dried fruits, nuts,
beans, and dairy products like milk, cheese, and yogurt—can
help prevent leg cramps. If you get a cramp, stay calm and then
pull your toes back toward you and push your heel away. This
stretches the muscles and releases the cramp.

SWELLING

Some women find that their shoes no longer fit. Swelling in
your feet, ankles, and legs is normal during pregnancy. As your
uterus gets bigger, there is pressure on the blood vessels in your
legs. Try to avoid standing for a long time, and when you sit or lie
down, put your feet up and don't cross your legs. Wear loose clothing that doesn't bind anywhere. Drinking lots of fluids will not
increase the swelling, but will actually help reduce it by keeping
your kidneys working well. If you see a big change in the amount of
swelling you have—including in your face and hands—or if you
have a sudden weight gain, call your health care provider right away.

Is it normal for my feet to swell like this?

LEAKING BREASTS

Your breasts are getting ready to feed a baby, and may leak a
yellowish or clear liquid called **colostrum** toward the end of your
pregnancy. This is normal but can be embarrassing. A cotton
cloth or pad in your bra will absorb the leaks. Wash the dried
liquid from your nipples with plain warm water, not soap.

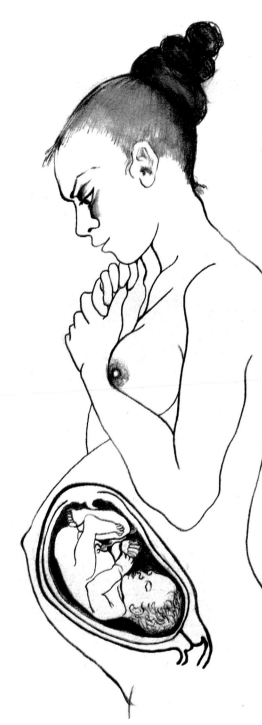

"Full Term" 36 to 40 Weeks

Although we talk about pregnancy taking 9 months, a full-term baby is in the womb close to 10 months. Just before birth, the baby is fully formed and ready to move into the birth canal.

GETTING READY FOR BABY

THERE MAY BE a lot to do before your baby arrives. You will want
to have a place for your baby to sleep, blankets, diapers, clothing, a car seat, a stroller . . . the list can seem very long.

Childbirth classes are recommended during the last trimester.
You and your partner—or whoever will be your labor coach—
will learn what to expect when your baby is born, and you'll meet
other people who are going through the same thing. Classes
remind you that there are still decisions to be made, such as:

- **If my baby is a boy, should he be circumcised?**
- **Should I breastfeed?**
- **If I'm going back to work soon after my baby is born, who
will I find for daycare?**

This is a good time to get information about these choices.
Ask your health care provider about circumcision, and do some
reading as well. Your health care provider may direct you to a
breastfeeding specialist (called a lactation consultant) or classes,
so you can feel more comfortable about breastfeeding even
before your baby is born. Tour daycare centers now, or visit the
home where you will leave your baby while you work. Get a
sense of what kind of care is given to the other children and see
if that feels all right to you.

If you haven't selected a health care provider for your baby
yet, now is the time, so that he or she can begin taking care of
your baby in the hospital.

Being prepared can help you feel more relaxed. Freeze some
extra meals so you won't have to worry about cooking when you
come home with a new baby. Stock up on supplies for yourself,
such as maxipads, nursing bras, compresses that can be heated or
chilled, and supplies for your baby.

If you're planning to use disposable diapers, expect to use 8
to 10 diapers a day, and have at least a week's worth of the
smaller-sized disposables ready for your newborn.

If you're going to use cloth diapers and wash them yourself,
think about how often you want to wash diapers. About 4 dozen

*What do I do to get
ready for the baby?*

will keep you from having to wash diapers every day in order to have a good supply of clean ones. If you are using a diaper service, the service will provide you with the necessary amount.

For your baby's first clothes, get simple, inexpensive shirts, nightgowns, and infant suits. You will be surprised at how quickly your baby will outgrow the first clothes. You probably will change your baby's clothes 2 or 3 times a day, so you may want to have enough clothes that you will not need to wash every day.

Showers, garage sales, and hand-me-downs are good ways to get the supplies you need. Be sure, however, that any used equipment meets federal safety standards.

You will need a federally-approved infant car seat as soon as your baby is born if you are planning to take him or her home from the hospital in a car.

ADOPTION

IF YOU ARE placing your baby for adoption, it is important to have a general plan in place so that your hospital stay will be easier. If you have not done so already, the beginning of the last trimester of your pregnancy is when you should work with a social agency or lawyer to learn about your options for placing your baby with a family.

What if I'm placing my baby for adoption?

Some questions to consider include:

- **How much contact do I want to have with my baby during my hospital stay?**
- **What kind of family will I want to care for my baby?**
- **What feelings do I have about placing my baby in another family's care?**
- **How will I say good-bye to my baby? Or will I continue to have contact?**

Talk with your health care providers about your adoption plans so they can support you in the last months of pregnancy, both in the hospital and during the first weeks at home. This may be a difficult time for you. Talking about your feelings and decisions with others can help.

PRETERM LABOR

LABOR is considered "preterm" if it occurs more than 3 weeks before your due date—or before 37 weeks of pregnancy. Not all preterm labor means a premature birth. Often labor can be stopped, and the baby can be given more time to develop and grow before birth.

What if my baby is born prematurely?

If you have vaginal bleeding or fluid leaking from the vagina, you should call your health care provider immediately. Other symptoms of preterm labor are sometimes hard to recognize because they are like the normal discomforts of pregnancy. Often the only difference is how strong the symptom is, how regularly it occurs, or how long it lasts. Be aware of these signs of possible preterm labor:

- **Change in vaginal discharge.** If the discharge is watery or bloody, call your health care provider immediately.
- **Increased pelvic pressure, for an hour.** This is a very heavy feeling, as if your baby is pushing down, in your back, thighs, and lower abdomen.
- **Cramps, like menstrual cramps, for an hour.**
- **Dull backache below the waistline, for an hour.** Most women have some backache during pregnancy. A low backache that comes and goes but doesn't go away when you change position may be a sign of preterm labor.
- **Five or more contractions or feelings of tightening in an hour.**
- **Intestinal cramps, for an hour.** There may be diarrhea, but not necessarily.
- **"Something doesn't feel right" or "something feels different."** Trust your instincts and call your health care provider.

If you have any of these symptoms, empty your bladder, drink a glass of water, lie down on your side for an hour, and feel for contractions or other symptoms. Time the contractions. If you have had 5 or 6 during the hour, or you still have other symptoms, call your health care provider.

How to Help Prevent a Preterm Birth

- **Drink 8 to 10 glasses of liquid every day.** Water, milk, and juices are best. Don't drink more than 2 or 3 caffeinated drinks, like coffee or cola, a day.
- **Prevent and treat constipation.**
- **Empty your bladder frequently.**
- **Decrease stress in your life.**
- **Avoid strenuous activities if they cause contractions.**
- **Stop smoking.**
- **Do NOT prepare your nipples for breastfeeding.** Some books recommend this, but the stimulation can bring on early labor.
- **Report signs of a bladder infection to your health care provider.**
- **Eat regular, nutritious meals.**
- **Be aware of contractions and warning signs.** If you notice tightening or other symptoms, do the following for 30 minutes:
  - Lie on your left side with a pillow behind your back for support.
  - Place your fingertips on your abdomen.
  - If your uterus feels tight and hard, like a clenched fist, and then gets soft again, you are having a contraction.
  - Keep track of the time from one contraction starting to the next one starting. (See page 61 for information on how to time your contractions.)

It's normal to have some contractions during pregnancy, but more than 5 or 6 in an hour is too many, and you should call your health care provider.

If you are at risk for preterm labor, your health care provider may give you more specific instructions.

CLINIC VISITS

AROUND YOUR eighth month of pregnancy, you will begin seeing your health care provider every other week. During the last month, these visits will be every week. Partners are encouraged to attend these visits, too.

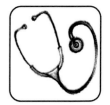

How often will I see my
health care provider?

The usual weight and blood pressure measurements will be taken, and your urine and blood will be checked. Your health care provider will listen to your baby's heartbeat and measure the baby's growth.

If your blood is Rh-negative, at about the beginning of the seventh month of pregnancy, or 28 weeks, your health care provider will recommend that you have an injection of RhoGAM. This will prevent your body building up antibodies against your baby, in case your baby's blood is Rh-positive.

Pelvic examinations by your health care provider during the last month or so of your pregnancy can help determine when your baby will be born. As you approach the baby's due date, the cervix gets thinner and begins to open. This is called effacement (thinning) and dilation (opening). You may hear your health care provider say things like "You're 30 percent effaced," or "dilation is one centimeter."

GESTATIONAL DIABETES SCREENING

Gestational diabetes occurs in up to 12 percent of all pregnancies in the United States and can be a concern for the health of both the mother and the baby. If it's diagnosed early, complications during the pregnancy can be prevented.

Before your visit, the clinic nurse will give you instructions about the test, which is usually done at 28 weeks. At the clinic, you will be given a sugar solution to drink and then, an hour later, a blood sample will be taken. The results are often ready immediately. If the blood sugar results are high, further testing may be done.

FOR PARTNERS

GETTING READY for the baby is something the two of you can do together. Paint a bedroom, look for a crib, gather the supplies you will need when the baby arrives.

It can be fun to cook together, preparing meals that you can freeze and use during the first weeks after the baby is born. You are likely to find yourself very busy when the baby arrives, just like your partner. She'll need a certain amount of tending—and so will the baby. Even if you're a wonderful cook, you may find yourself out of time, and those prepared meals will come in handy.

Ask your partner what you can do for her: perhaps rubbing her back, shopping for groceries, or bathing the other children.

Learn everything you can at childbirth classes, and make sure that both of you practice the breathing and relaxation exercises you are taught. There's a temptation to think you don't have to practice, that it will all come naturally, but it will be much better for both of you if you know what you're doing.

Visit the place your baby will be born with your partner. Find out what you can bring to make labor and birth more comfortable.

FOR MORE INFORMATION

A Child Is Born by Lennart Nilsson.
Active Birth by Janet Balaskas.
The Birth Partner by Penny Simkin.
Essential Exercises for the Childbearing Year by Elizabeth Noble.
Pregnancy, Childbirth, and the Newborn by Penny Simkin, et al.
Pregnancy Day by Day by Sheila Kitzinger and Vicky Bailey.
While Waiting by George E. Verrilli, MD, and Anne Marie Mueser.
Your Premature Baby by Frank Manginello and Theresa Foy
    DiGeronimo.

Childbirth.org <www.childbirth.org>.
Fairview Health Services <www.fairview.org>.
International Childbirth Education Association <www.icea.org>,
    1-800-624-4934.
Lamaze International <www.lamaze-childbirth.com>,
    1-800-368-4404.

Keeping Track of Your Pregnancy

The following pages are a place for you to write down thoughts, events, and changes during your pregnancy. Some of the pages can be used to help you and your health care provider work together; others let you remember your hopes and dreams about your baby.

CLINIC VISITS

USE THIS SPACE to record each visit to your health care provider (make photocopies of this page as needed).

Date of visit: _____ Weight: _____

Tests done: _____

Your questions and your health care provider's comments:

_____

_____

Date of visit: _____ Weight: _____

Tests done: _____

Your questions and your health care provider's comments:

_____

_____

Date of visit: _____ Weight: _____

Tests done: _____

Your questions and your health care provider's comments:

_____

_____

Date of visit: _____ Weight: _____

Tests done: _____

Your questions and your health care provider's comments:

_____

_____

Date of visit: _____ Weight: _____

Tests done: _____

Your questions and your health care provider's comments:

_____

_____

Date of visit: _____ Weight: _____

Tests done: _____

Your questions and your health care provider's comments:

_____

_____

YOUR BABY'S MOVEMENTS

AT THE START of your third trimester, counting your baby's movements will help reassure you about your baby's well being. Choose the time of day when your baby is likely to be most active. Follow these steps at the same time every day:

    1. Write the time you begin on the record below.

    2. Lie down on your left side.

    3. Count 10 baby movements (rolls, kicks, and so forth). Do not count hiccups.

    4. On the record below, note the time that your baby has completed 10 movements.

    5. Smoking is not recommended during pregnancy. If you smoke, do not have a cigarette for at least one hour before counting your baby's movements.

WHEN TO CALL YOUR HEALTH CARE PROVIDER

- If it takes more than one hour to feel 10 movements.
- If there is a change in the normal pattern of your baby's movements.
- If there is a sudden increase in wild movements followed by the absence of movement.

Date	Start time	End time	Minutes to feel 10 movements	Comments

Preferences for Your Baby's Birth

BE SURE to inform your health care providers about your preferences before you go into labor.

What would you like the medical care staff to know about you?

_____

_____

Describe some of your fears and concerns about labor and delivery.

_____

_____

During the first stage of labor, what are your preferences for:

Managing comfort:

_____

_____

Medical interventions:

_____

During the second stage of labor, what are your preferences for:

Managing comfort:

_____

_____

Medical interventions:

_____

What other things are important to you about your birth experience?

_____

Describe your preferences in case of an unexpected event (such as cesarean birth, complicated or prolonged labor, or problems with the baby).

_____

PREFERENCES FOR YOUR BABY'S CARE

BE SURE to inform your health care providers about your preferences before your baby is born.

Describe any fears or concerns you may have for your baby.

_____

_____

_____

_____

_____

What would you like to feed your baby?

___ Breast milk   ___ Formula

Are there any exams or procedures that you would prefer your baby to have (or not have)?

_____

_____

_____

What kind or instruction or information would you like to receive at the hospital (baby care, breastfeeding, and so forth)?

_____

_____

_____

If you have a baby boy, what are your wishes regarding circumcision?

_____

What other things are important to you regarding your baby's care?

_____

_____

Your Support System after Birth

Be sure to include names and phone numbers, and don't be afraid to ask for help.

Which of the following professionals might you consult after your baby is born?

Childbirth educator/breastfeeding educator

_____

Physician/nurse-midwife

_____

Doula/postpartum support person

_____

Lactation consultant

_____

Postpartum support group leader

_____

Who among your friends and relatives can help you after you leave the hospital?

_____

What can your friends and family do to help (for example, with meals, errands, laundry, transportation, and so forth)?

_____

_____

_____

Who do you trust to care for your baby so you can rest for an hour or two?

_____

Who can you call when you need someone to talk to?

_____

Who can your partner call on for help and support?

_____

_____

Your Baby Arrives

Giving birth can take days, or just a couple of hours. Every woman's experience is different. And if you've had more than one baby, you know that even for the same woman, each birth is different. With the help of your partner, support persons, and health care providers, you can go into child-birth feeling confident.

SOME OF THE QUESTIONS ANSWERED IN THIS CHAPTER INCLUDE:

- How will I know if I'm in labor?
- What do "dilation" and "effacement" mean?
- What happens during the transition phase?
- What is the afterbirth?
- What happens with a cesarean birth?
- What kind of exercise can I do after having a baby?
- What if I don't feel overwhelming love for my baby right away?
- Why do I feel sad?

BEFORE LABOR

EVERY LABOR and birth are different, but there are some conditions that may indicate a baby is ready to be born. Any or all of the following may occur before the start of labor.

How will I know if I'm in labor?

- **Lightening or engagement.** The baby drops deeper into your pelvis, usually about 2 to 4 weeks before delivery. You may notice that you are able to breathe more easily and you'll have less heartburn, but you may have more lower back pain and you may find yourself making more trips to the bathroom.
- **Diarrhea or loose, frequent stools.**
- **Burst of energy.** Women call this the nesting instinct. Suddenly you're cleaning house, getting the baby's room ready, or cooking up a storm. Enjoy this burst of energy, but don't overdo it and tire yourself too much.
- **Large increase in vaginal discharge.** Discharge or mucus, called a **mucus plug**, may be pink or brownish. This discharge may be seen as long as 3 weeks before labor begins—or on the same day.
- **Low backache.** Use the pelvic rock exercise (see page 12) to stretch out your back. Warm baths, hot water bottles, or back rubs also help.
- **Softening of the cervix.** Your health care provider will notice this during a vaginal exam.
- **Rupture of "bag of waters."** Amniotic fluid may either leak or gush out. It's usually clear and odorless, and you may mistake it for urine at first. You should call your health care provider immediately if your water breaks. Note the time you noticed the liquid, the amount, and the color (clear, brown, yellow, green, or pinkish) to tell your health care provider.
- **Contractions begin.** Regular contractions that get longer and stronger (more painful) as time passes are an important sign that labor has begun.
- **Cervical effacement and dilation.** The most reliable sign that labor is under way is the thinning and opening of your cervix. This can be seen only in a cervical exam.

CONTRACTIONS

A contraction sometimes feels as if your lower abdomen has become a tight fist. (Bend your arm and "make a muscle" on your upper arm. Feel this muscle. This is what a contraction in your abdomen will feel like if you put your hand on it.) The contraction will loosen, then tighten a few minutes later. You may feel a dull ache in your back, coming all the way around to the front of your abdomen and down your thighs. In early labor, contractions usually feel like strong menstrual cramps.

Contractions are caused by the muscles at the top of your uterus tightening and pulling up the lower part of your uterus, making the cervix open, and then pressing the baby down through the cervix.

TIMING CONTRACTIONS

You will need to time your contractions. This means keeping track of how long they last and how often they happen.

Duration, or how long a contraction lasts, is timed from the beginning of a contraction to the end of that same contraction. It's usually measured in seconds.

Frequency, or how often contractions occur, is timed from the *beginning* of one contraction to the *beginning* of the next contraction. It's measured in minutes.

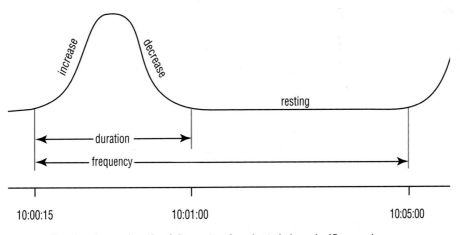

The duration, or length, of the contraction charted above is 45 seconds. The frequency, or time between the beginning of this contraction and the beginning of the next contraction, is 4 minutes and 45 seconds.

Pre-Labor

You may feel contractions but not be in labor yet. This **false labor** is actually the body getting ready for birth, so it's more accurately called **pre-labor**. In true labor, the time between contractions will gradually shorten, and the contractions themselves will strengthen. You may start out feeling contractions every 15 minutes; then after an hour you will realize they are coming every 10 minutes, and it takes more concentration for you to breathe through them and stay relaxed. Some women may start true labor with contractions that are strong right away and that come every 3 to 4 minutes.

Contractions in pre-labor don't come regularly and are likely to vary in strength. They may even weaken after awhile.

Walking is a good way to test whether you are in true labor. If your contractions get stronger as you walk around, you are most likely in true labor. If they go away or seem weaker as you walk, you are probably in pre-labor. Talking also helps test whether you are in true labor. If you can't talk while having contractions, it's likely to be true labor.

If you are still unsure, call your health care provider.

If You Think You Are in Labor

If you think you are in labor, your health care provider will want to talk to you about whether you should come to the hospital. The tone of your voice gives your health care provider important information about your labor.

Questions your health care provider may ask include:

- **Has your water broken?**
- **Have you noticed an increase in vaginal discharge?**
- **How regular and close together are your contractions?**
- **When did your contractions start? When did they become regular?**
- **How are you feeling?**

LABOR AND SPIRITUALITY

AS YOU PREPARE for the birth of your baby, you may experience many thoughts and emotions. Excitement, apprehension, and uncertainty may mingle with joyful anticipation of finally holding your baby in your arms. Many women feel that they are joining with a creative power much larger than they are. Some call this power God or Allah, the Creator or Higher Power. Regardless of your religious tradition, you may well see childbirth as a sacred or holy event and feel the need to draw profoundly upon your faith for strength and guidance.

During labor, you may choose a ritual such as a sacred reading, prayer, or song. If you would like help from the hospital staff for this ritual, ask your nurse for assistance. You may also consider asking someone to be with you during labor to give spiritual support. A special object with spiritual significance may also be brought to your hospital room. Finally, many families wish to choose a song, prayer, or special reading to welcome the new baby into the world. All of these things can help you find closure as one phase of your life ends—and find blessing as another phase begins.

BREATHING AND RELAXATION

LEARNING HOW to breathe and relax properly can make your labor a much easier experience. Childbirth classes are an excellent place to learn and practice breathing and relaxation, even if this isn't your first baby. If you haven't taken childbirth classes, you can still use breathing and relaxation techniques—and the nurses helping you will be able to support you.

If you want to have a labor and delivery without pain medication, you may want to identify strategies for dealing with pain and practice these ahead of time with your partner or support person. Even if you plan on using pain medications, proper breathing and relaxation techniques will help you before you are given medication, or if the medication doesn't help as much as you expected.

BREATHING BASICS

Breathing gives you and your baby oxygen. Comfortable, relaxed breathing during labor helps the uterus work more effectively and the cervix open more easily.

- **Remember to keep breathing.** It's a normal reaction to hold your breath if you feel pain, but breathing through the discomfort will help. Breathe at a rate and depth that make you feel relaxed and comfortable. This may vary throughout labor.
- **Finding a focal point, something to look at and concentrate on, may be helpful.** This focal point might be nothing more than a spot on the wall; some women use a favorite photo or small item that they bring to the hospital with them. Other women prefer to look inward to concentrate.
- **Use a cleansing breath before and after each contraction.** "Cleansing breath" simply means inhaling deeply and exhaling slowly.
- **Try to relax between contractions.** You may change the pace and style of your breathing to help you cope in labor. Listen to what your body is telling you, and your health care providers will assist and support you.

Some breathing techniques that women have used in
labor include:

- **Slow-paced breathing.** This is like an extension of the
  cleansing breath, from deep in your chest. Just take easy,
  deep breaths and release them slowly.
- **Steady-paced breathing.** These are shallower breaths from
  your chest. Say the word "hee" in order to keep your breaths
  coming at an even pace.
- **Varied-paced breathing.** You can time these breaths—
  especially with a birth partner's help—by counting a series of
  "hees" ending with a puff. For example: "hee, hee, hee, blow."
  You can make yourself concentrate more on your breathing
  by varying the pattern: "hee, hee, hee, blow—hee, hee,
  blow—hee, blow—hee, hee, hee, blow," etc. Your partner
  can help you vary the pattern.
- **Breathing with the pushing urge.** You may have an overwhelming urge to push, even before it's time for the baby to
  be born. This urge may feel as if you need to move your
  bowels. Pushing often against a cervix that isn't fully open
  can cause the cervix to swell. To control this urge, you can
  keep repeating any word, "pant," or make short bursts of air
  as if you're trying to blow hair off your forehead.

Illustrated below are some positions you may want to try when you are in labor—or when you just need to relax. Remember to use a variety of positions and to change positions frequently.

Positions for Relaxation or Labor

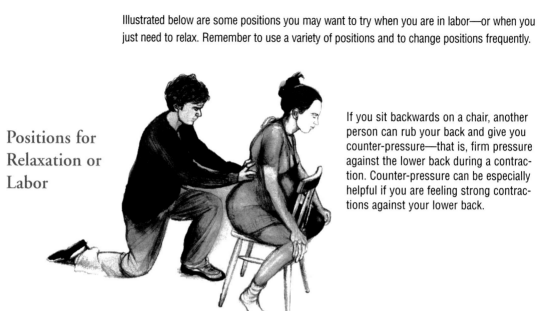

If you sit backwards on a chair, another person can rub your back and give you counter-pressure—that is, firm pressure against the lower back during a contraction. Counter-pressure can be especially helpful if you are feeling strong contractions against your lower back.

The side-lying position, with pillows to support your head and leg, can help you relax comfortably during contractions.

Getting on your hands and knees can help with labor pains in your lower back. It helps relieve the pressure of the baby's head on your tailbone. When you are in this position, another person can rub your back or give you counter-pressure. This position also may allow the baby to move into a better position for delivery.

RELAXATION BASICS

You can use relaxation techniques all of the time, not just in labor. You'll find they help in many situations, from going to the dentist to coping with the demands of your new baby. There are a number of things you can do to make relaxing easier.

- **Get comfortable.** Wear comfortable, preferably loose, clothing. Sit or lie in a position where you won't feel pinched. Seek quiet places. Listen to soothing music.
- **Practice regularly.** Practice relaxation techniques at least three times a week. Do it at the same time, whether that's early morning or before you go to bed.
- **Tell your partner what helps you relax and what distracts you.**
- **Pay attention to the parts of your body that react to stress.** Does your neck ache? Do your legs get stiff?
- **Think of yourself in a calm place, where you are feeling peaceful.** Imagining that you are relaxed may help you be relaxed. Some people find it helpful to imagine themselves in a particular place—lying on a warm beach, walking in a quiet forest, sitting on a mountaintop—that means "peace" to them.

Staying as relaxed as possible will help you feel more comfortable and may make your labor move along more quickly. Ways to stay relaxed include going for a walk, getting a massage, taking a warm bath or shower, "slow dancing" with your partner, or even humming or moaning a "labor song."

Many women feel that a rhythmic activity like swaying or rocking in a rocking chair is relaxing. Remember to breathe at a comfortable depth and rate.

Your partner can help you by encouraging you to relax and breathe properly and by caressing you while supporting your body.

LABOR AND CHILDBIRTH

THERE ARE three stages of labor, and three phases—early, active, and transition—during the first stage. (For specific information on each stage of labor, see the charts on pages 76 and 77.)

FIRST STAGE OF LABOR

During the first stage of labor, the opening to your cervix is thinning out (effacing) and opening up (dilating) so that your baby can be born. The thinning, or **effacement**, is usually described in percentages. If your health care provider says you are 50 percent effaced, it means that the cervix has thinned to half its normal thickness. The opening, or **dilation**, is usually described in centimeters—10 centimeters would be fully dilated.

For some women, effacement and dilation may start days before they are ready to give birth, and proceed very slowly. For others, it may happen in a matter of hours.

Your health care provider may refer to **station**, or how low your baby is in your pelvis. When the baby's head is engaged at **zero station**, your baby is ready to move through the pelvic opening.

What do "dilation" and "effacement" mean?

Effacement

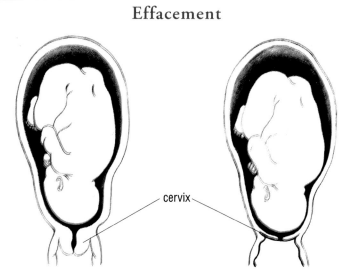

cervix

The mother's cervix "effaces," or thins, as the body prepares for birth. The illustration on the left shows a cervix that is not effaced yet, although the baby's head is pushing down. The cervix on the right is fully, or 100 percent, effaced.

Early Phase

When your labor begins, you may feel excited and relieved that it's finally time to have the baby. A warm bath, a cup of tea, a walk, slow dancing, or a massage may help you relax, and your partner can help you with these. Every woman is different, so pay attention to what makes you feel most comfortable.

Stations of Engagement

The baby's head is "engaged" when it is deep in the pelvic cavity. This illustration shows the "stations" of engagement. When the head is fully engaged, it is at zero station.

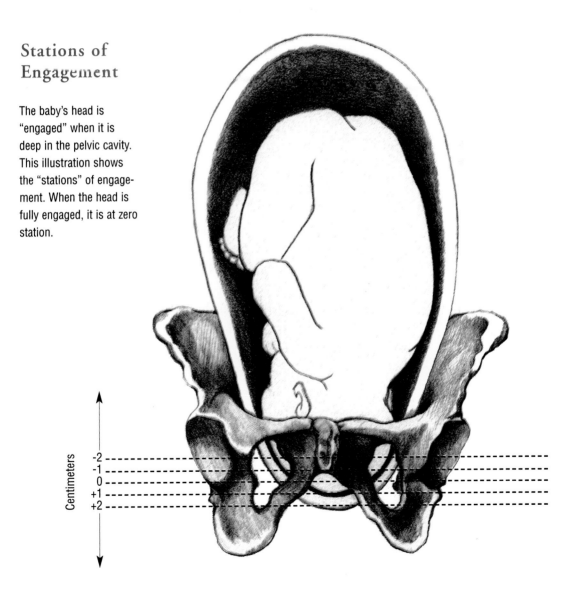

Active Phase

In active labor, your contractions will become longer, more painful, and closer together. You may feel nauseated, restless, and more inwardly focused.

When the contractions are strong and frequent, it's normal to feel a little doubt about whether you can handle even stronger and more frequent contractions. Use whatever breathing seems to work. Just remember to keep breathing and to use the relaxation techniques you learned in class and have been practicing at home.

Transition Phase

As your cervix dilates from 8 to 10 centimeters, your contractions will become quite strong, one right after another. You may be restless, perspiring, nauseated, hot, cold, or tense. Your body is working hard, and it takes a lot of effort to stay calm and to breathe through the contractions.

It may be hard for you to listen to what your health care providers are saying right now. You are very focused on getting through each contraction.

This is the hardest part of labor for many women. You may worry that you can't keep going. It *will* be over soon. It may be helpful to remember that every contraction brings you closer to being done with labor and able to see your new baby.

Your birth partner and your health care providers will be supporting, encouraging, and calming you during this difficult stage. If you have practiced your relaxation and breathing exercises, you may find it easier to cope right now.

As the transition phase ends, you may begin to feel like pushing or bearing down, rather than continuing your regular breathing. Tell your birth partner and health care provider when you have this feeling. Your birth partner can help you with breathing the short puffs that help prevent pushing before it is time.

Comfort Management

During labor, many women feel more comfortable when walking, pelvic rocking, taking baths or showers, and using breathing techniques. However, some women may need some kind of medication to help them stay focused and relaxed.

What happens during the transition phase?

Medications you might receive during labor and delivery include **sedatives, systemic analgesics** (pain relievers), **intrathecal analgesia, epidural analgesia**, or **general anesthesia.** All of these medications have benefits and drawbacks. The chart here gives you an idea of what these medications are.

TYPE	BENEFITS	DRAWBACKS
Sedative	Can relieve tension and help with rest and relaxation. Sometimes given early in labor to help a tired mother sleep. Helps relieve nausea and vomiting.	May cause dizziness, disorientation, dry mouth, or a drop in the mother's blood pressure.
Systemic Analgesics (Pain relievers)	Lessens pain and can help relaxation. Given during active labor.	May slow labor. If given too close to delivery, may cause slow breathing, poor sucking, or decreased muscle tone in newborn. This medication is unlikely to be used during transition or pushing.
Intrathecal Analgesia	A small amount of medication is injected into the spinal area by the anesthesiologist. Pain relief is often immediate and thorough. There is no numbing, so mother can be active after the injection. Pushing urges are felt.	May cause itching, nausea, or urinary retention in the mother. Medication can help control side effects.
Epidural Analgesia	Similar to intrathecal analgesia. A catheter is inserted into a space around the spine. Medication may be given all at once or continuously. Provides thorough pain relief.	I.V. fluids are given. The mother is numb from naval to mid-thigh and likely to stay in bed after injection. Decreased urge to push, which may result in use of forceps or vacuum extractor. Electronic fetal monitoring must be used.
Spinal Anesthesia	Used only for cesarean birth. Produces complete numbness from breastline to toes. Mother will be awake and comfortable for the birth.	May cause a drop in mother's blood pressure, nausea, or vomiting. Side effects for mother may be relieved with medication.
General Anesthesia	Used for fast cesarean delivery in case of emergency. Given by injection or inhalation. Mother quickly becomes unconscious.	Nausea or vomiting may occur. Mother not awake for birth. May cause respiratory distress, less vigorous suck, or poor muscle tone in baby for a short time after birth.

SECOND STAGE OF LABOR

In this stage, you begin to push and deliver your baby.

Once your cervix is fully opened, you may feel an overwhelming urge to push, as if your body is making all the decisions and the rest of you is just following along. This is hard work, but it can also be a relief: NOW you're going to have the baby.

Pushing often feels like having a very large bowel movement—and the pushing itself can sometimes cause you to have one. Don't worry about it; this is normal and may be a sign you are pushing well.

With help from your birth partner and health care providers, find a position that feels comfortable while you push. If you squat or stand, gravity will help the baby descend as you push, but for some women, squatting or standing is too hard on their legs. You may sit, in a regular chair or on a special birthing stool. If you want to lie down try lying on your side, with your upper leg supported by your birth partner, rather than on your back.

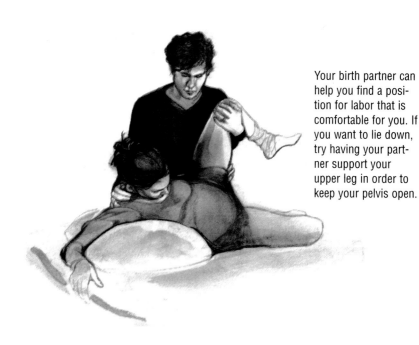

Your birth partner can help you find a position for labor that is comfortable for you. If you want to lie down, try having your partner support your upper leg in order to keep your pelvis open.

Once you have begun serious pushing, things may move fairly quickly. You are so focused on pushing and having this baby that you may barely hear what anyone says to you, and you will not pay much attention to anything else going on in the room.

Pushing time for a woman having her first baby is usually one to two hours. It's about a half hour less for women who have already had at least one baby.

In a normal birth, the baby will be born head first. The top of the head will begin to show as you push with contractions. **Crowning** is when the widest part of the baby's head is out of your body.

If an **episiotomy**—a surgical cut to enlarge the birth opening—is needed, it's done as the baby's head crowns. An episiotomy can help the baby be born faster, if there is some difficulty in the birth process. Many women can give birth without tearing or an episiotomy.

After the baby's head is delivered, the shoulders will emerge. Then the rest of the baby's body almost slips out.

Your health care provider will clamp and cut the umbilical cord that connects your baby to the placenta. (Often your birth partner will be offered the opportunity to do this.)

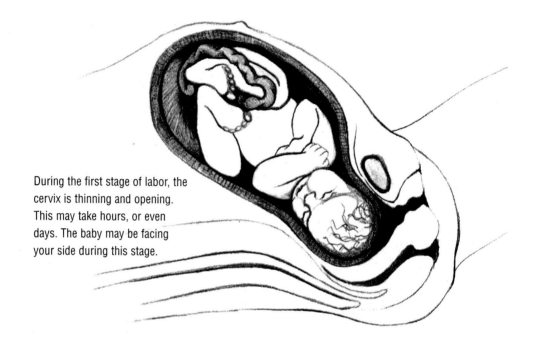

During the first stage of labor, the cervix is thinning and opening. This may take hours, or even days. The baby may be facing your side during this stage.

The top of the baby's head shows, or "crowns," as you push. Usually, the baby is facing your spine as it is being born.

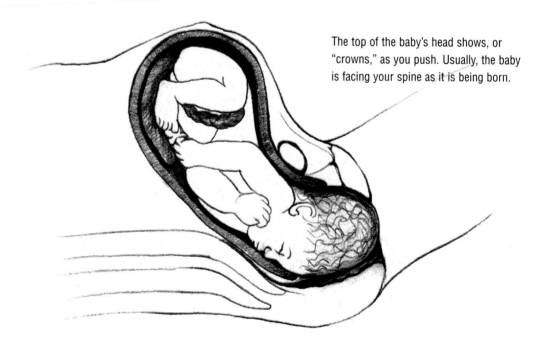

In most births, the baby's head is delivered first, and takes the most effort.

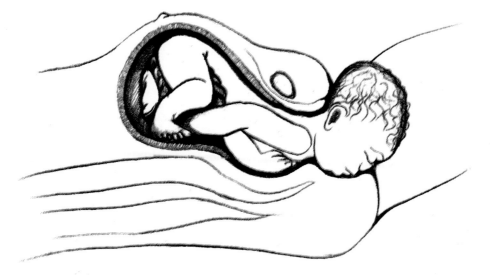

Once the head and shoulders are delivered, the rest of the baby's body comes out easily.

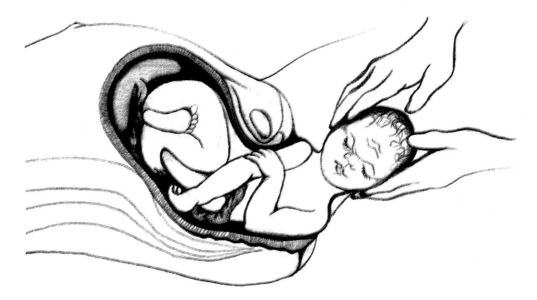

LABOR AND DELIVERY

FIRST STAGE: Dilation and Effacement of the Cervix (4-20 hours)

PHASES	LENGTH[1]	CONTRACTIONS	POSSIBLE EMOTIONAL, PHYSICAL SIGNS	PARTNER'S ROLE	COMFORT MEASURES
Early Dilation 0-4 cm Effacement 0-60%	1st baby 8-10 hours 2nd+ baby 4-6 hours	Intensity: mild Length: 30-45 seconds Interval: 5-20 minutes (irregular)	Abdominal cramps Intensity increases when activity increases Backache Bloody show Leak or rupture of BOW[2] Diarrhea Excitement Anxiety	Entertainment Help with relaxation Prepare for hospital trip Time contractions Keep calm Notify midwife/doctor Back pressure	Maintain normal activity as possible Bath or shower Comfortable position Pelvic rocking Back pressure Light diet Standing/walking
Active Dilation 4-8 cm Effacement 60-100%	1st baby 3-6 hours 2nd + baby 2-4 hours	Intensity: more painful, closer and longer Length: 50-60 seconds Interval: 2-5 minutes	Pain/pressure in hips, groin, back of legs Hot flashes/chills Increased bloody show Leak or rupture of BOW Thirsty Nausea, vomiting Harder to relax More quiet, "inward focus" Restless Feeling dependent	Stay close and calm Help with relaxation Time contractions Encourage position changes Wipe forehead with cool cloth Offer ice chips/fluids Constant encouragement After each exam, ask about progress Consider bath/shower Foot rubs, massages Help establish/protect rituals	Rituals Rhythmic movement Relaxation Empty bladder Change position Pelvic rocking Suckers/hard candy/popsicles Cool cloth Backrub Slow chest breathing Focal point Consider medication
Transition 8-10 cm	1st baby 1/2-3 hours 2nd+ baby 1/2-2 hours	Intensity: very strong Length: 70-90 seconds Interval: 1 1/2 to 2 min.	Very hard contractions Amnesia between contractions Leg cramps Backache Urge to push Nausea and vomiting Chills/hot flashes Shaking of legs Demanding, exhausted, vulnerable, scared, panicky	Offer encouragement Breathe with mom Backrub Supply dry pads Time contractions Simple clear directions Acknowledge her pain, have confidence that she can cope Notify staff if she wants to push	Take one contraction at a time Position changes/relaxation Backrub Cool cloth/fanning Ice chips/sips of water Socks/warm blanket Be open to support from caregiver and partners

[1] Lengths of time are averages. Your labor may be faster or slower and still be normal.
[2] BOW = "Bag of waters," or amniotic membrane.

SECOND STAGE: Delivery of Baby

LENGTH	CONTRACTIONS	POSSIBLE EMOTIONAL, PHYSICAL SIGNS	PARTNER'S ROLE	COMFORT MEASURES
1st baby ¹/₂-3 hours 2nd+ baby ¹/₂-1 hour	Intensity: may be mild at first, increased intensity over time Length: 60 seconds Interval: 3-5 minutes	Urge to push/rectal pressure Backache Stretching, burning, stinging sensation in perineum Confusion Fatigue	Help with position/body support Fan mom Cool cloth, ice chips Encourage relaxation between contractions Praise mom Prepare camera, etc. Ask to assist with delivery or cut cord, if you wish Enjoy birth	Listen to your body's urges Relax pelvic floor Adjust position for comfort, effective pushing Look at or touch baby's head Work with caregivers Pant to avoid pushing, or push as directed to do so Cool cloth, ice chips

THIRD STAGE: Delivery of Placenta

LENGTH	CONTRACTIONS	POSSIBLE EMOTIONAL, PHYSICAL SIGNS	PARTNER'S ROLE	COMFORT MEASURES
2-45 minutes	Intensity: usually mild (contractions may be stronger with 2nd+ baby) Length: irregular Interval: irregular	Relief May cry Desire to hold baby or simply rest	Praise mom Hold and enjoy baby Encourage mom to relax Look at placenta if desired Share in the joy and excitement	Push as directed to birth the placenta Breastfeeding Relax and rest Hold baby, if desired

FOURTH STAGE: Recovery

LENGTH	CONTRACTIONS	POSSIBLE EMOTIONAL, PHYSICAL SIGNS	PARTNER'S ROLE	COMFORT MEASURES
1-2 hours	Intensity: mild Length: short Interval: irregular	Relief, happiness Abdominal cramps (especially when breastfeeding) Lochia (blood discharge) Hunger, thirst Dizziness Curiosity about baby	Be proud of yourself and mom Telephone calls to family and friends Share feelings about the birth Help position baby for nursing Enjoy closeness with mom and baby Help screen visitors and calls	Breastfeeding Sponge bath Ice chips on bottom Food Position changes Rest and relaxation

THIRD STAGE OF LABOR

What is the
afterbirth?

The **placenta**, often called the **afterbirth**, is expelled a few minutes after your baby is born. You will have a few contractions, usually painless. Your health care provider will watch for signs that the placenta is ready to be delivered and may ask you to push a little to help expel it. As the placenta is expelled, you may feel pressure.

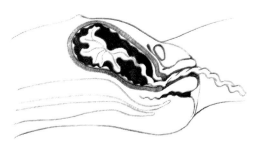

The placenta is delivered shortly after the baby is born.

Immediately after Birth

Health care providers attending the birth will suction the baby's nose and mouth gently if needed and will make sure your baby is breathing well. The baby will be placed on your abdomen so you can see, touch, and bond with your new child. Often the baby is placed at your breast to begin nursing.

If you have had an episiotomy or a tear in your perineal area, your health care provider will stitch you up after the delivery of the placenta. You will be given a local anesthetic similar to Novocain so you will not feel the stitching.

Apgar Score

A quick rating, called the **Apgar score,** is given right at birth, then again 5 minutes later, to measure how well the baby is doing after labor and delivery. The baby is given a "score" of 0 to 2 on five different aspects of its condition: heart rate, breathing, muscle tone, skin color, and reflex response.

CESAREAN BIRTH

A CESAREAN BIRTH—often referred to simply as a **cesarean**—may be needed if the baby is in an abnormal position or if the mother or baby show signs of problems during labor. Your health care provider will help you decide whether a cesarean is necessary.

Once the decision to proceed with a cesarean is made, you will be moved quickly to an operating area.

During a cesarean, a doctor makes an incision in your abdomen and into the uterus and then removes the baby through the incision. In most cases, you will have regional anesthesia that numbs you but does not put you to sleep. If the doctor feels your baby needs to be delivered very quickly, you might be given general anesthesia, and you will not be awake as the baby is born.

After the birth, your uterus and then your abdomen will be stitched closed by the doctor.

Your birth partner will usually be able to be with you during the cesarean, if the hospital and your health care provider allow it—and if your birth partner is comfortable with the idea.

Because of the skill of the doctors and nurses, and the use of modern medical equipment, most mothers and babies do well after the operation. Your recovery will be slower than it would be after a vaginal birth; you have just had abdominal surgery, and those tissues and muscles need time to heal again.

If you've been planning for a vaginal delivery, you may feel that a cesarean is somehow a "failure." This just isn't true. A cesarean can quickly relieve problems you or your baby may be having during the birth process. Except in rare emergencies, you and your birth partner will be fully involved in deciding whether to have a cesarean. A cesarean may offer the best opportunity for you and your baby to have a safe and healthy birth.

Having a cesarean doesn't necessarily mean that your next baby will have to be delivered by cesarean, too. You should discuss vaginal birth after cesarean (VBAC) for your next pregnancy with your health care provider.

What happens with a cesarean birth?

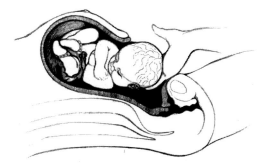

In a cesarean, the baby is delivered through an incision in the abdomen and the uterus. Except in an emergency, the mother can be awake during the birth, and a partner may be present.

MEDICAL PROCEDURES DURING LABOR AND BIRTH

PROCEDURE	BENEFITS	DRAWBACKS	WHAT YOU CAN DO
Intravenous Fluids (I.V.) A thin catheter is inserted into a vein in the mother's arm. Fluids or medicines are given through this catheter.	Provides quick access to mother's circulation for fluids or medications May help mother keep fluids in her system if she is vomiting Can help control blood pressure if regional anesthesia is given	May restrict movement during labor May cause pain at insertion site during or after labor May be unnecessary if mother is drinking adequate fluids	Ask care provider if you can take fluids by mouth instead Ask for a saline lock (provides access to a vein but does not restrict movement) If you are confined to a bed or chair, change positions every 20-30 minutes Ask staff about reasons for intervention
External Electronic Fetal Monitoring (EFM) Two instruments, held in place by elastic belts, are placed on the mother's abdomen. Using ultrasonic waves, one instrument records the baby's heart rate, and the other records the mother's uterine contractions.	Can provide useful information about baby's condition and tolerance of labor May be helpful in certain medical procedures (such as pitocin use) May be less limiting to mother's mobility than internal monitor Noninvasive; no risk of infection	May restrict movement during labor Not always accurate; may require further intervention to assess baby's condition May lead unnecessarily to further medical interventions Not proven to provide clear benefits to mother or baby in low-risk labor	Listening to the baby with a Doppler instrument may be an option in certain circumstances If you are confined to a bed or chair, change positions every 20-30 minutes Ask staff about reasons for intervention
Internal Electronic Fetal Monitoring (EFM) Two instruments are used to measure uterine activity and baby's heart rate. The instrument used to assess the baby is inserted through the cervical opening and attached to the baby's scalp. The other instrument is threaded through the vagina to rest along the uterine wall.	Is more accurate than external EFM Can provide useful information about baby's condition and tolerance of labor May be helpful in certain medical procedures (such as pitocin use) May be less limiting to mother's movement than external EFM	Invasive; may present risk of infection to mother and baby Requires the rupture of amniotic membrane May restrict movement during labor May lead unnecessarily to further medical interventions Not proven to provide clear benefits to mother or baby in low-risk labor	External monitor, fetoscope, or Doppler instrument may be an option in certain circumstances If you are confined to a bed or chair, change positions every 20-30 minutes Ask staff about expected length of labor if membranes need to be ruptured Ask staff about reasons for intervention
Episiotomy A surgical incision in the perineum to enlarge the vaginal opening for birth or the use of instruments for delivery. Repair is done after birth of placenta.	Can speed delivery by 15-20 minutes for exhausted mother or distressed baby May help when baby is very large or instruments are used to assist birth Provides "straight" incision, which may be easier to repair than some large tears	Causes pain in early postpartum period May result in a more extensive tear than if episiotomy is not done Repair can interfere with early interaction with baby Extension of the incision can result in damage to rectal tissue	Ask care provider in advance about his or her common practice regarding episiotomy If desired, state your wish to be asked permission for procedure beforehand Seek pain medication, ice packs, perineal pads, or sitz baths as needed Ask staff about reasons for intervention

PROCEDURE	BENEFITS	DRAWBACKS	WHAT YOU CAN DO
Instrument Assistance for Birth • Vacuum Extraction (VE): A cuplike device placed on the baby's head and held in place by suction pressure. • Forceps: Spoonlike instruments placed one at a time around the baby's head.	Can assist in vaginal birth when mother is exhausted or baby is not in good birthing position May be necessary when mother has had regional anesthesia and cannot feel her pushing contractions Can speed delivery if baby is in distress	VE may cause bruising and swelling on baby's scalp VE may not be as helpful in rotating baby as forceps Forceps may cause tissue damage on baby's face and/or mother's vagina Both procedures may require episiotomy	Discuss your concerns about these procedures with your care provider ahead of time Ask staff about reasons for intervention
Cervical Ripening A medication (usually a synthetic hormone) is placed near the cervix and allowed to act on the cervical tissue.	Can begin labor contractions Can make pitocin more effective for induction by promoting cervical "ripening"	May not work to ripen cervix	Ask about alternatives for ripening cervix (nipple stimulation, sexual intercourse, and so forth) Ask staff about reasons for intervention
Amniotomy An instrument called an amnihook is inserted through the cervix and used to snag the amniotic membrane. The membrane then breaks.	May help start or speed the process of labor by starting or increasing the strength of uterine contractions May be necessary to assess the color or consistency of the amniotic fluid May be necessary when inserting an internal electronic fetal monitor	May increase risk of infection for mother and baby Staff may feel an increased sense of urgency about the birthing process in order to decrease risk of infection May not be effective in starting or speeding labor; may lead to other interventions May limit mother's ability to use bathtub/shower for comfort during labor Will likely produce more painful (though more effective) contractions	Ask about alternatives to start or speed labor (nipple stimulation, shower or bath, walking, and so forth) Ask staff about expected length of labor if membranes are ruptured Ask staff about reasons for intervention
Induction/Augmentation of Labor A synthetic hormone (such as pitocin) is given through an I.V. line. This may cause contractions to begin or become stronger.	Can help begin labor if baby is overdue or if complications have developed that may necessitate birth of the baby Can help strengthen contractions, thus making them more effective	Close observation of mother and baby (with external or internal EFM) is required Requires I.V. line, which limits mother's mobility during labor Contractions may be more painful or closer together May result in premature birth if done without knowledge of baby's maturity	Ask about alternatives to stimulate labor (nipple stimulation, shower or bath, walking, and so forth) If movement is limited, change positions frequently Negotiate for more time, if desired Review coping strategies for I.V. line and monitors (page 80) Ask staff about reasons for intervention Ask for a telemetry (remote) procedure for EFM

Your Hospital Stay

YOU MAY STAY in the hospital only a couple of days, but even a short stay should be as comfortable as possible. Sleep and rest are very important after you've delivered your baby. You may feel excited and wide awake for a while, but remember that your body has been working hard and needs time to recover.

If you have visitors in the hospital, try to keep their visits short and don't feel that you have to entertain them.

Safety and Security

You, your baby, and your birth partner will have been "banded" right after birth, with matching identification bands attached to your wrist and your baby's wrist or ankle. The bands will be checked frequently while you are in the hospital.

Incidents are extremely rare, but for security reasons do not hand your baby to anyone in the hospital who doesn't identify himself or herself and who isn't wearing an identification badge. If you have any hesitation or doubts, call for a nursing supervisor.

Your baby may stay in the room with you—keeping your baby with you as much as possible will help you learn more about the baby—but if you leave the room, even just to take a quick shower, do not leave the baby alone.

Hospital Routines

During your hospital stay you can expect that:

- **Several nurses will care for you, as work shifts change every 8 to 12 hours.** They will check on you a few times each day. They also will help you with breastfeeding and give you information about caring for yourself and your baby at home.
- **Someone from the lab will draw blood from you and your baby.**
- **Your health care provider will visit you several times during your stay and talk to you about when you can go home.**
- **Your baby's health care provider will examine your baby several times, talk with you, and decide when your baby can go home.**
- **A representative from a photography firm may talk to you about ordering photos of your baby.** This is optional; you do not have to buy any photos.

- If you have Rh-negative blood and received Rhogam at about 28 weeks of pregnancy, you may receive another injection before you leave the hospital.
- If you are not immune to rubella (German measles), you will have a shot to protect any future babies.

POSTPARTUM CARE

AFTER YOUR BABY is born, your body begins its recovery. It doesn't recover all at once, but it does change noticeably right away. Just as you paid attention to the needs of your body during pregnancy, it's important to pay attention to those needs now.

ACTIVITY

Rest is very important. Your baby's needs will disrupt your sleep during a time when you could use a little more sleep than usual. Let other people—your partner, your mother, friends, relatives—help you.

You can do many of your daily activities at home, but do them one by one. Give yourself time for naps during the day when your baby is sleeping. Avoid lifting anything heavy or doing strenuous work or sports.

If you had a cesarean birth, you may be advised to avoid vacuuming, driving, or climbing stairs for 2 to 3 weeks.

VAGINAL FLOW, MENSTRUATION

Right after a vaginal birth, your vaginal flow will be bright red. It should become dark red before you leave the hospital. If you see large clots (bigger than half dollars) or smell a bad odor, be sure to tell the nursing staff.

Your vaginal flow may continue for 4 to 6 weeks after you give birth. Usually the amount decreases and the color turns brownish-red, then white or clear. If you have been too active, your flow may become a brighter red and grow heavier for a while. If you need more than one pad an hour, lie down, rest, and call your clinic.

Menstrual periods usually start again 6 to 8 weeks after delivery. If you are breastfeeding, your periods may be delayed. You can still get pregnant, however.

PERINEAL CARE

Use the peri-bottle you got in the hospital and change sanitary pads every time you go to the bathroom. Take as many warm tub baths as you like to ease any pain. Do not use tampons or douches until vaginal bleeding has stopped.

INCISION CARE

After a cesarean birth, you can shower, but try to keep water off your incision. If the "steri-strip" tapes on your incision come loose, you can take them off after you've been home for a week. Gently pull both ends of the strip toward the incision. You may see a small amount of clear or pink drainage. Check with your health care provider if the drainage increases or has an odor, if the incision reddens, or if you have a fever.

BOWELS/HEMORRHOIDS

Reduce your risk of constipation, which is common after childbirth, by drinking plenty of fluids—6 to 8 glasses of non-caffeinated liquids every day—and by increasing the amount of fiber in your diet. If hemorrhoids are a problem, warm tub baths are soothing. Try not to strain when you have a bowel movement. Your health care provider can recommend an over-the-counter medication to help with constipation.

NUTRITION

Keep up the good eating habits you developed during pregnancy. Eat a well-balanced diet that includes foods from every part of the food pyramid (see pages 8 and 9). Don't try to lose your pregnancy weight quickly by cutting back on calories.

KEGELS

Those Kegel exercises you were doing during pregnancy are still useful. (In fact, they are useful throughout your life.) After having a baby, you may barely be able to feel the muscles, but if you keep doing the Kegels, you are less likely to leak urine when you sneeze or cough.

SEX

Sexual intercourse should be avoided for at least 3 to 4 weeks after delivery, or until the brownish-red vaginal flow is completely gone. Most health care providers recommend that you not have vaginal intercourse until after your post-delivery clinic visit. If you do, however, and you do not want to become pregnant again, you should use birth control. It's possible to get pregnant within a month after having a baby, even if you're breastfeeding.

WHEN TO CALL YOUR HEALTH CARE PROVIDER

- If you have a temperature of 100.4° F or higher.
- If you have heavy vaginal bleeding, bright red bleeding saturating more than one pad an hour, or clots larger than a half dollar.
- If you have bleeding for more than 6 weeks.
- If you have burning or pain while urinating, or a frequent or urgent need to urinate.
- If you have pain in one spot or a red area on your breast.
- If you have foul-smelling vaginal discharge.
- If you have increased drainage, swelling, pain, or redness around your incision from a cesarean birth.
- If you have redness or pain around a vein in your leg, or if you can't stand on that leg.
- If you have extreme abdominal pain.

EXERCISE

YES, YOU CAN start exercising soon after birth, but most health care providers recommend waiting about 6 weeks before starting any serious workouts. Begin exercising slowly, but make exercise a part of your daily routine. Remember, it took you months to gain your pregnancy weight and shape, and it will take months to lose them.

What kind of exercise can I do after having a baby?

Start walking, a little bit at a time. This will help you feel better in general, although it won't work on specific muscles like the exercises described below.

ABDOMINAL TIGHTENING

Lying on your back or side (or, later, sitting or standing), take a deep breath in through your nose and feel your abdomen expand. Blow the air out slowly through your mouth while pulling your abdominal muscles in. Do this 2 to 3 times to start. You can do this exercise 24 hours after birth.

PELVIC TILT

Lie on your back with your knees bent. Flatten your lower back against the floor. While letting your breath out, tighten your abdominal muscles and then hold for 3 to 4 breaths. Relax and repeat.

YOUR EMOTIONS

ALMOST ANYTHING you feel after your baby is born is normal—that is, other women often feel the same way.

You may feel an instant connection to your baby, but don't worry if you don't. For many women, the love and connection grows as they take care of their new baby for days or even weeks.

In the first 24 hours after birth, you will start learning how to take care of yourself and your baby: how to change diapers, how to give your baby a bath, and how to feed your baby. You may still be thinking about your labor and delivery. It can be hard to believe that your pregnancy is over and you actually have a baby now.

After a day or so, you will feel the bond between you and your baby strengthening. You begin to see your baby as a separate person, with a special personality and needs.

BABY BLUES

Many women find themselves feeling some amount of sadness and anxiety from 3 to 10 days after delivery. They may feel tired, irritable, sad, or confused. They may even feel guilty—"I have a wonderful baby, why do I feel so sad?"

It's normal to feel blue. Your hormones are rapidly returning to pre-pregnancy levels, you are tired, and you aren't getting enough sleep. Having a baby, especially a first baby, changes your life. If you were working before the birth, now you may feel lonely being at home with just your baby for company most of the time.

The important thing is to talk to others: your partner, relatives, friends, your health care provider. Ask for help so you can get more rest and feel more confident about taking care of your baby.

What if I don't feel overwhelming love for my baby right away?

Why do I feel sad?

POSTPARTUM DEPRESSION

If you feel blue for more than a few days—or if at any time you feel as if you are out of control and may harm yourself or your baby—get help right away. Call your health care provider. Postpartum depression is real and can be serious.

ADOPTION

If you placed your baby for adoption, you may feel a strong sense of grief after the birth. You may have sad feelings on holidays, birthdays, or even during a diaper commercial. Give yourself a chance to rest and heal. Ask your health care provider, social worker, or adoption agency for support groups or agencies that can help you express and accept your feelings of sadness and support you in your decision.

CLINIC VISITS

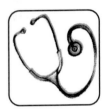

YOU WILL BE asked to see your health care provider 2 to 6 weeks after giving birth. At this visit, you may have some blood drawn and your urine tested, and you'll have a physical, including a pelvic exam. If you have not had a Pap smear for a year or more, your health care provider will take one.

At the exam, your health care provider will discuss family planning options with you and will answer any questions you have about exercise and other physical activities.

As noted earlier, most health care providers recommend that you not have vaginal intercourse until after your post-delivery clinic visit. If you do, however, and you do not want to become pregnant again, you should use birth control. It's possible to get pregnant within a month after having a baby, even if you're breastfeeding.

FOR PARTNERS

YOUR HELP is essential throughout the birth process—and maybe even more important afterwards. The birth of a baby is an exciting and wonderful time for both you and your partner. There is nothing quite like the experience of welcoming a new little person into the world.

If you've gone through childbirth classes with your partner, you already know what you can do during labor and birth: helping with breathing, saying encouraging words, giving massages, supporting her as she gets into position to deliver the baby.

Maybe this makes you a little nervous. After all, you've probably never been present for a birth before. What if you faint? What if you can't handle it? It's normal to be nervous. If you have very strong fears, talk with your partner long before the baby's due date so you have a back-up plan, such as another relative or friend to be a birth partner if needed.

You and your partner may want to consider hiring a professional support person, called a **doula**, to help with labor. A doula is specially trained to assist women and their partners before, during, and after birth. The doula is not there to take your place but rather to help you and your partner during this important event. For a list of doulas in your area, check the Yellow Pages or ask your childbirth educator or health care provider.

Your partner will need a lot of support after giving birth. She's still recovering physically, and she also needs emotional support. She may get the "baby blues," and she can use some reassurance from you. After the birth you can help by burping the baby, changing diapers, giving the baby a bath, and so on. If she is breastfeeding, your encouragement and support will mean a great deal to her. You and your partner can share caring for the baby, delighting in every little thing he or she does.

FOR MORE INFORMATION

SEE THE list of resources at the end of the previous chapter.

Index

diabetes, 51
diapers, 14, 47, 48, 86, 87, 88
diaphragm, 44
diarrhea, 49, 60
diet, 3, 8–10, 15, 29, 35, 37, 84
dilation of cervix, 51, 59, 60, 68
disposable diapers, 47
doula, 2, 58, 88
domestic abuse, 17–18
douche, 27, 84
Down syndrome, 19, 39
drainage from incision, 84
drugs, 5, 8

early phase, 68, 69
effacement of cervix, 51, 59, 60, 68
egg, 22–23
electronic fetal monitoring. *See* fetal monitoring.
embryo, 21, 23
emotions, 14–16, 20, 28, 37–38, 63, 86–87
engagement, 60, 69
epidural analgesia, 71
episiotomy, 73, 78, 80–81
esophagus, 35
exercise, 3, 11–13, 15, 20, 26, 28, 35, 40, 45, 52, 59, 60, 70, 84, 85–87

faintness during pregnancy, 24, 26–27
fallopian tube, 23, 29
false labor, 62
family practice physician, 4
father. *See* partner.
fetal alcohol syndrome, 7
fetal monitoring, 71, 80–81
fetus, 23, 34
fever, mother's, 19, 84
first stage of labor, 56, 68–71, 74

first trimester of pregnancy, 21–32, 35, 37
Food Pyramid, 8–9, 84
forceps, 71, 81
formula, 57
frequent urination, 24, 27, 43
full-term baby, 42, 46

general anesthesia, 71, 79
genetic counseling and testing, 19
genetic disorder, 19
genitals, 16
gestational diabetes, 51
getting ready for baby, 47–48, 52, 62
growth and development, 30

headache, 18, 27
health insurance, 6, 31
heartburn, 35, 60
hemorrhoids, 45, 84
hepatitis, 29
high blood pressure, 27
HIV, 29
hormones, 14, 26, 35, 36, 81, 86
hospital routines, 82–83
hospital stay, 1, 31, 48, 82–83
human chorionic gonado-tropin (HCG), 39

ibuprofen, 27
identification of baby, 82
incision, 79–80, 84–85
induction of labor, 81
insurance. *See* health insurance.
intrathecal analgesia, 71
intravenous fluids (I.V.), 71, 80
iron, 29

Kegels, 11, 27, 45, 84

second stage of labor, 56,
    72–77
second trimester of pregnancy,
    17, 33–40
sedative, 71
sex and sexuality, 3, 17, 20,
    28, 79, 84–85
shoulder rotation, 13
sibling, preparation of, 33, 38
side-lying position, 66
skin, baby's, 9, 34, 78;
    mother's, 24, 36, 39
sleep, baby's, 47; mother's, 15,
    35, 37, 71, 79, 82,   83, 86
smoking, 7, 50, 55
sneezing, mother's, 11, 36, 84
sperm, 22–23
spina bifida, 19
spirituality, 16, 38, 63
spotting, 28
stages of labor, 68–81
station, 68–69
stress, 11, 15, 38, 50, 67
stretch marks, 36
suppositories, 27
swelling, 18, 36, 45, 81, 85
systemic analgesics, 71

tailor sit, 12
tampons, 84
temperature, mother's, 85
third stage of labor, 78–81
third trimester of pregnancy,
    15, 17, 41–53
tiredness, 24, 26, 33
transducer, 30
transition phase, 59, 68, 70, 71
triple screen test, 39
Tylenol, 27

ultrasound, 19, 30, 39
umbilical cord, 34, 42, 73
unconjugated serum estriol,
    39
urination, 18, 24, 27, 43, 71, 85
urine, 4, 11, 19, 27, 29, 39,
    43, 51, 60, 84, 87
uterus, 25, 27, 29, 34, 36,
    42, 43, 45, 50, 61, 62,
    64, 79

vacuum extractor, 71, 81
vagina, 17, 18, 24, 27, 28, 31,
    45, 49, 60, 62, 79, 80–81,
    83, 84, 85, 87
vaginal birth after cesarean
    (VBAC), 79
vaginal bleeding, 17, 18,
    28–29, 49, 84, 85
vaginal discharge, 18, 24, 27,
    28, 49, 60, 62, 85
vaginal flow, 83, 84
vaginal infection, 17, 27
vaginal or abdominal pain, 17,
    18, 85
varicose veins, 43
vernix, 34
visits to the clinic, 3–5, 29–30,
    39, 40, 51, 54, 87
vomiting, 18, 24, 71, 80

what's happening to your
    body, 24–27, 35–36,
    43–46

your baby's development,
    22–23, 34, 42

zero station, 78–69